MEXICAN AMERICAN BASEBALL ON THE WESTSIDE OF LOS ANGELES

Portrait of a "Bonus Baby"

In 1958, Richard "Buzzy" Hernández smiles confidently in his Orioles uniform, the Stockton sun pounding down. Deep furrows wrinkle his brow. Does he squint to ward off the afternoon glare or to disguise the angst of disappointing family, friends, and the entire Westside of Los Angeles, whose dreams ride on his 20-year-old shoulders?

Down on one knee, a bat rests on his thigh, both his hands lightly holding the Louisville Slugger. Beneath his wool Orioles jersey, he wears an undershirt, the colored sleeves cut at the elbows, probably with scissors, like his father, Rufino, taught him.

Having spent three years in second-class buses and cheap hotels, he's played with Orioles farm teams from Bisbee, Arizona, to Aberdeen, South Dakota, to Paris, Texas, and Arkansas to Winnipeg, where he met Janet, the pretty girl in the bleachers, to whom he made a promise to return.

In California again, home barely 200 miles away, his fate rests with the Stockton Ports. In high school, he blasted homers in ballparks across Los Angeles; now, he is one bright star among many.

Does he recall the night he signed the $25,000 contract—an incentive to join Baltimore, a "bonus baby," as the local media dubbed him? His parents, family, and agent beamed; José Alfredo Jiménez smiled from his mother Carmen's favorite record.

My cousin's portrait stands prominently in our living room. LA's Westside kids take up bats, balls, and gloves to follow him, like he followed his father, a 1939 semipro in Santa Monica, until Hitler, Mussolini, and Hirohito intervened.

Are those furrows on his brow permanent?

Triumph is close, maybe a season away, but home is also close, a short jaunt south down Highway 101.

—Daniel Cano

Front Cover: Ray Serra was a baseball ringer from Santa Monica playing shortstop and third base. He broke his leg in multiple places while he was being recruited by the New York Yankees and Pacific Coast League scout Bill Essick, thus ending his aspirations of being a professional ball player. (Courtesy of the Serra family.)

Cover Background: The 1940s Santa Monica team included Félix Guajardo (third row, far right), who sports a band-aid on his nose after breaking it during a league game. Two sets of brothers played on this team, Félix and Ángel Guajardo and Manuel and Ray Serra. (Courtesy of Ray Romo.)

Back Cover: Rick Prieto (left), from Culver City, and Víctor Prieto, from San Pedro, California, met in 1981 when they played for the Rojos de Caborca. Although not related, Víctor always enjoyed telling people that he and Rick were *hermanos* (brothers). In 1982, they played for rival teams—Rick for the Diablos Rojos del México and Víctor for the Tigres del México. (Courtesy of Rick Prieto.)

MEXICAN AMERICAN BASEBALL ON THE WESTSIDE OF LOS ANGELES

Richard A. Santillán, Christopher Docter, Alicia S. Stevens, Ray P. Serra Jr., and Rebecca García-Prieto
Foreword by Dan Guerrero

ISBN 978-1-4671-0331-2

Published by Arcadia Publishing
Charleston, South Carolina

Library of Congress Control Number: 2019941224

For all general information, please contact Arcadia Publishing:
Telephone 843-853-2070
Fax 843-853-0044
E-mail sales@arcadiapublishing.com
For customer service and orders:
Toll-Free 1-888-313-2665

Visit us on the Internet at www.arcadiapublishing.com

I dedicate this book to all the Mexicans and Mexican Americans who played professional ball, and to my wife, Teresa, my noble inspiration for writing these books.

—Richard

For all the amazing people I have gotten to know working on this book series. Your stories have given me a newfound appreciation and pride for the Valley, the place that I have called home all my life. Your friendship has enriched my life more than you know.

—Chris

To our father, Ray Serra, who now plays baseball inside the pearly gates. May your passion for baseball be instilled in your grandchildren in whatever endeavors they pursue.

—Alicia and Ray

To my husband, Richard (Rick), for your unwavering strength of character, respect, knowledge, and love of baseball, which you exemplify in your coaching every day. I am proud of you. And to our daughter Sandra, for your love, encouragement, support, and sacrifice for your father's coaching career, we thank you. God's blessings and my love to you both.

—Becky (Rebecca)

CONTENTS

ACKNOWLEDGMENTS

The coauthors are indebted to the players, families, community members, and organizations for their remarkable photographs and amazing stories, including Jesse Sánchez, Jesse Plasencia Jr., Culver City High School, Dale Súchil, Henry "Hank" Ynostroza Jr., Carlos Salazar, Sergio Hernández, Marcelino Saucedo, Joe Romero, John Lemos, Charles and Sandy Santillán, Stephanie Santillán Ramírez, Bea Amenta Dever, Alex Nuñez, the Leopoldo Sánchez family, Donavan López, John Fraire, Marge Villa, Frank Botello, Angelica Félix, Vince García Sr., Pedro Garza, Tommy Gómez, Fabiola González, Manuel Guajardo, Sal Hernández, Carlos Meléndez, Dan Meléndez, Roger Packard Jr., Tommy Rivera Jr., Mike Rivera, Raymond Romo, Raúl Sáenz, Michael Serra, Martha Guajardo Shaw, Ron Vincent, Hope Santellano Alcalá, Alice Almeida, Margaret Pérez Amescua, Rudy Aragón, Danny Argott, Jo Argott, Marie Armenta, Connie Ávila, Ray Barraza, Ray Barraza Jr., Kristy S. Bórquez, Robert Bórquez, Danny Bórquez, Bob Calzada, Josephine Cancino, Lorrie Carrillo, Joe Casillas, Art Castañeda, Rámona Valenzuela Cervantes, Rosie Díaz, Richard Díaz, Virginia Ruiz Durazo, Richard F. Encinas, Joe Escalante and family, Amador Espinoza, Robert Estrada, John Fonseca, Mary Gallegos, Richard Gallegos, David García, Gerald García, Irene García, Jim García, Joffee García Jr., Pinney García Jr., Speedy Gonzáles, Liz González, Joe Govea, Terry Hernández, Efrénia Hidalgo, Mike Hidalgo, Rachel Jiménez, Marianne Castro Lawson, Bobby Luján, Adela Almeida Madrid, David Magaña, Beverly García Manasse, Arnold Murillo, Mary Murillo, Mary Jane Muro, Vickie Carrillo Norton, Laura Ochoa, Robert Ochoa, Della Fonseca Ortega, Mike Palacios Jr., Abel Pérez, Tommie Pérez, Reggie Ponce, Pete Prieto, Mike Ramírez, Rosie Alderete Rico, Raymond Rivera, Irene Rodríguez, Everto Ruiz, Tony Servera, Naomi Talamantes, Mike Velarde, Robert Villanueva, Sylvia Valencia Wiltz, John Romero, Juan Cueva, Robert Estrada Jr., Jess Trejo, Gilbert Gómez, Irene Vaiz, Héctor Zamora, Canoga Park Guadalupe Community Center, Canoga Park Historical Society, Pacoima Historical Society, San Fernando Valley Historical Society, Monse Segura, Elisa Grajeda-Urmston, and our editor Jeff Ruetsche.

The coauthors salute three special individuals for their remarkable contributions to this publication. Richard (Rick) Prieto contributed pictures and personal stories covering his love of playing baseball in high school, college, the professional Mexican leagues, and over 40 years of coaching. He is currently the head baseball coach at Culver City High School. Daniel Cano has authored three novels and has been recognized with several literary awards. He has held administrative positions at UCLA, UC Davis, and CSU Dominguez Hills, and retired from Santa Monica College. Dan Guerrero is from Wilmington, where he played basketball and baseball. He attended UCLA on a baseball scholarship and was inducted into the UCLA Hall of Fame in 1996. He has served as the athletic director at UCLA since 2002. In 2017, he was a finalist for Athletic Director of the Year by *Sports Business Journal/Sports Business Daily*.

FOREWORD

Growing up in Wilmington, California, a blue-collar community in the heart of the Los Angeles Harbor area, the most influential person in my life was my father, Gene Guerrero. He instilled in me a strong work ethic, a competitive spirit, and a love for music and sports. Baseball was my favorite sport to play, but I had a hard time hitting the pitching of the older kids I played against. I was frustrated, but my dad took the opportunity to make me focus on defense. I spent hours in my driveway working on drills, and before long, I was making diving plays no one else could make. My prowess as a shortstop became widely known around town. That's what's so great about baseball: it teaches you that you can always find a way to get better and that there's no shortcut to greatness.

Mexican American Baseball on the Westside of Los Angeles pays tribute to the personalities, teams, and events that shaped the course of baseball and softball history from the San Fernando Valley to Santa Monica, Venice, West Los Angeles, Culver City, and down to my hometown of Wilmington. My dad and I were huge fans of the Dodgers, and as a young baseball player, my biggest sports hero was Jackie Robinson. His accomplishments, both on and off the field, made my college decision easy. My dad would say that because of Jackie, UCLA was a "university for the people." What he meant was that a person who looked like me, a minority, would not only be accepted at UCLA, he could thrive and excel there. When I put on the UCLA baseball uniform for the very first time in the fall of 1969, the same uniform that Jackie wore, it was reverential. My passion for social and racial equality was founded as a young Latino growing up in Los Angeles and was further fueled by my time at UCLA and the connection I felt to Jackie.

I am proud to call the Westside home and to continue to support baseball and softball programs that will be as influential in the lives of today's youth as the sport of baseball has been in my own life.

—Dan Guerrero
Athletic Director
University of California at Los Angeles

INTRODUCTION

If Charles Dickens were alive today, he might have referred to the Westside of Los Angeles as a tale of two cities. This region includes extremely wealthy communities with some of the most valuable real estate in the world, including Beverly Hills, Bel Air, Malibu, Westwood, Santa Monica, and Pacific Palisades. It is not uncommon to witness multi-million-dollar homes alongside a growing homeless population. The Westside of Los Angeles consists of neighborhoods west of La Cienega Boulevard to the Pacific Ocean, south of the Santa Monica Mountains, and north of Los Angeles International Airport.

There is also a significant Mexican American presence on the Westside of Los Angeles. A significant influx of Mexican immigrants occurred in the 1920s due to the collapse of the Mexican economy, the violent Mexican Revolution, and existing family networks. These newly arriving families and single men settled in designated portions of Santa Monica, Venice, Mar Vista, Palms, Culver City, and the West Los Angeles area strictly bordered by Centinela Avenue, Pico Boulevard, Olympic Boulevard, and Sawtelle Boulevard. In Santa Monica, the demarcation lines were Twelfth Street to the west, Centinela Avenue to the east, Pico Boulevard to the south, and Santa Monica Boulevard to the north. Mexicans were nearly always assigned to blue-collar occupations, including nursery workers, gardeners, barbers, small business owners, and other jobs that did not require a formal education.

In addition to employment stratification, the rigid disparity of race and wealth is best exemplified by the enrollment in the area's high schools. In the 1950s and 1960s, school counselors routinely directed Mexican American students into the automotive, wood shop, and typing majors, deliberately steering them into an educational path of lower career earnings, thus perpetuating their working-class status. Only a few Mexican Americans were given college-track courses.

Since Mexican American families resided in the same neighborhoods due to strict institutional housing patterns, they started baseball and softball games, leagues, and tournaments, formal and informal. Players, coaches, teams, umpires, scorekeepers, ground crews, team moms, batgirls and batboys, sportswriters, and others brought and continue to bring immeasurable admiration, unbridled enthusiasm, and everlasting dignity to their communities. This publication represents a humble part of this surprising story.

Santa Monica

Santa Monica is a beachfront city in western Los Angeles County, bordered by the Pacific Ocean on the west, West Los Angeles on the east, Pacific Palisades to the north, and Venice to the south. Santa Monica was named after Saint Monica. In the 1870s, the Los Angeles & Independence Railroad Company connected Santa Monica with Los Angeles, increasing the number of visitors to the area, which ultimately led to increased population as visitors opted to remain. Santa Monica's close proximity to Los Angeles International Airport (less than eight miles), made it a destination for vacationers seeking beachside exposure.

With an ever-growing population, both commerce and recreational activities expanded. Douglas Aircraft Company (1922) the Rand Corporation (1945), and PaperMate (1957) were three of the city's major employers. Mexicans, however, were primarily gardeners, landscapers, or workers at the local nurseries. The famed Santa Monica Pier was built in 1909, followed by the wildly popular Pacific Ocean Amusement Park. During the early 1900s, Mexican immigration accelerated due to a poor economy and civil strife in México. Many Mexicans traveled north seeking employment and reconnection to family members. People of color were allowed to own or rent property only within certain areas of the city. Mexican Americans settled between Pico and Santa Monica Boulevards and from Twelfth Street up to Centinela Avenue, commonly known as the Pico District.

Along Olympic Boulevard from Fourteenth to Twentieth Streets, Mexican American businesses thrived, in the form of restaurants, bars, and *tortillerias*. Many of them, such as Martínez Market, Joe's Café, El Retoño, and the Casillas Market sponsored Mexican American baseball teams in Santa Monica. The Mexican American community became fragmented in 1966 when it was decided by the city, through eminent domain, that the Santa Monica Freeway should run through the middle of their already small community. Not having a voice in city government, many Mexican American families were displaced by the freeway and forced to relocate to outlying communities. St. Anne's Church and School were significant institutions for Mexican Americans in the area, serving as a center for all activities. For Mexican Americans, love of baseball developed at St. Anne's School through the Catholic Youth Organization, where baseball competitions took place between Catholic schools in the Los Angeles archdiocese. That love of baseball continued in adult recreational leagues at Memorial Park.

Santa Monica native and artist Daniel Alonzo painted this picture of his family's store, Casillas Market, on Olympic Boulevard. Olympic Boulevard was populated with Mexican businesses from Fourteenth to Twentieth Streets. This area was also known as "La Veinte" (the 20th). As seen here, the Santa Monica Freeway encroached on the business and residential district, resulting in the displacement of the Mexican community. Today, none of the businesses remain after the Mexican residents were forced to relocate to surrounding communities. (Courtesy of Daniel Alonzo.)

This 1939 Santa Monica Cafemen photograph, taken in front of team sponsor Joe's Café at Fourteenth Street and Olympic Boulevard, includes, from left to right, (first row) Mario Vásquez, Ray Serra, Rubén Bontty (batboy and Joe's Café owner's son), Félix Guajardo, Carmen Casillas, and Bud Boyce; (second row) Sam Bontty (manager), Ángel Guajardo, Vally Rivera, Pete Osti, Valentine Lugo, Gonzalo Mireles, Ralph Hernández, and Joe Bontty (owner of Joe's Café). The team won second place in the city championship. (Courtesy of the Serra family.)

The Santa Monica Cafemen softball team is pictured at Municipal Park (now known as Memorial Park) in Santa Monica in 1939. From left to right are (first row) Gonzalo Mireles, Ray Serra, Ángel Guajardo, Rubén Bontty (batboy), Bud Boyce, and Pete Osti; (second row) Sam Bontty (manager), Ralph Hernández, Carmen Casillas, unidentified, Valentín Rivera, Mario Vásquez, and Valentine Lugo. Not pictured are Larry Alcalá, Alex Casillas, Félix Guajardo, "Champ" López, and Tony Ramos. (Courtesy of Martha Guajardo Shaw.)

This 1938 team with unmarked uniforms might have been sponsored by Cycle and Sport Shop. The players are unidentified with the exception of Ángel Guajardo (first row, second from left), Ray Serra (second row, far right), and Benny Tapia (first row, far left). The Cycle and Sport Shop lineup included Carmen Casillas, Ray Serra, Ángel Guajardo, Félix Guajardo, Alex Casillas, Pete Osti, Mario Vásquez, Valentine Lugo, and Gonzalo Mireles. (Courtesy of the Serra family.)

This 1940s St. Anne's School baseball team featured, from left to right (first row) Vicente ?, Ernest Afner, Vince García, Rudy Burgos, Manuel Guajardo, Albert García, and Raúl Galván; (second row) Inéz Guerrero, Frank Ramos, Rudolf Chavira, Raúl Arambula, and Sister Philomena. Frank Ramos, approximately 13 years old here, after competing in Catholic Youth Organization baseball and completing his military obligation, played on many Mexican Santa Monica recreational teams before volunteering over 50 years of coaching at St. Anne's School. (Courtesy of Vince García Sr.)

This 1940s Santa Monica team includes, from left to right, (first row) Elías Casillas, Manuel Serra, Larry Alcalá, Sammy Romo, Ray Serra, and Art Lamorie; (second row) Willie Hernández, unidentified, Ángel Guajardo, Goy Casillas, Mario Vásquez, and Manuel Vega; (third row) Benny Tapia, two unidentified, Gus Mondine, and Félix Guajardo (with a broken nose). Two sets of brothers played on this team: Ray and Manuel Serra and Ángel and Félix Guajardo. (Courtesy of Ray Romo.)

Manuel Serra (left) and Ángel Guajardo of the Santa Monica team are seen in the early 1940s. Baseball in Santa Monica was played at Municipal Park at Fourteenth Street and Olympic Boulevard, adjacent to the Mexican businesses along the boulevard, such as Casillas Market, El Retonio, Martínez Market, and Gallegos Tortilleria, which sponsored many teams. Today, these businesses are gone. The baseball field remains active, though it is now referred to as Memorial Park. Equipped with lights, it continues to host recreational night games. (Courtesy of the Serra family.)

The 1946 Flowermen were sponsored by Paul J. Howard Nursery. Pictured at Memorial Park are, from left to right, (first row) Richard Hernández (batboy); (second row) Ray Serra, Rufino Hernández, Félix Guajardo, Davey Robertson, Sammy Romo, and ? Alcalá; (third row) Manuel Serra, Fred Rivera, John Hogue, Frank Talamántez, Ángel Guajardo, Pete Osti, and unidentified. Ray Serra met his future wife, Evangeline, at the nursery in 1946. (Courtesy of Martha Guajardo Shaw.)

The 1947 Flowermen team was sponsored by Paul J. Howard Nursery. From left to right at Memorial Park are (first row) Ralph Hernández, Ángel Guajardo, Sammy Romo holding son Ray Romo, Davey Robertson, Mario Vásquez, and Ray Serra holding son Manuel Serra; (second row) Fred Rivera (manager), Frank Ramos, John Pakes, Frank Casillas, Rudy Pakes, Manuel Serra, and Lewis Leyvas. Years later, Ray Serra's son Ray Jr. married manager Fred Rivera's niece Marion. (Courtesy of the Serra family.)

This 1949 Santa Monica AMVETS team includes, from left to right, (first row) Ángel Guajardo, Frank Casillas, Manuel Serra, Sammy Romo (with son Ray Romo in front), Socorro Casillas, and Rufino Hernández; (second row) Mario Vásquez, Larry Báez, Carmen Casillas, Félix Guajardo, Vince Mutaw, Ray Serra, and Fred Rivera (manager). Their season ended with 24 wins and no losses. (Courtesy of the Serra family.)

The 1950 Olympic Merchants (also known as the Olympians) won 22 of their 24 games. Pictured behind home plate at Memorial Park are, from left to right, (first row) Mattie Velásquez, Ray Serra, Larry Alcalá, Sammy Romo, and Manuel Serra; (second row) Frank Casillas, Rudy Pakes, Socorro Casillas, Ángel Guajardo, and Fred Rivera (manager). (Courtesy of the Serra family.)

Playing with a 1952 San Fernando Missions semipro team, Ray Serra swings at the ball. According to his son Manuel, Ray played on different teams during the week and on Sundays. He later umpired at Memorial Field, the same park where he had played most of his games. The catcher is Joffee García. (Courtesy of the Serra family.)

The 1952 San Fernando Missions team included, from left to right, Ray Serra, Art Magaña, Joffee García, and unidentified. Ray Serra, Ángel Guajardo, Ralph Hernández, Sammy Romo, Mario Vásquez, and Frank and Socorro Casillas were Santa Monica players selected to paid positions on the Missions team. Before freeways, these players were among the first carpoolers, traveling hours to the San Fernando Valley. (Courtesy of the Serra family.)

Frank Ramos often demonstrated baseball techniques to his teammates. At this 1948 practice, Frank shows Sammy Romo how to slide, while Sammy shows Frank how to straddle the bag. Their practice was held at Vets Stadium, near the West Los Angeles Veterans Administration. Imagine Frank's surprise when, after the passing of Monsignor Cyril J. Wood in 1987, he found over 70 years of photographs tossed into the trash. Frank recovered those photographs and auctioned them, raising money for the parish. (Courtesy of Ray Romo.)

Players for the 1958 Los Amigos Little League Braves (from left to right) Phillip Joseph Mondine, Peter Hernández, and Tommy Rivera stand in the front yard of Tomás Rivera's home on Raymond Street in Santa Monica. Danny Rivera is the little boy standing in front, suited up and ready to go. Mondine's father, Gus Mondine, played on the early 1940s Santa Monica team. (Courtesy of Tommy Rivera.)

The 1960 Los Amigos Park Western Boys League Braves are, from left to right, (first row) Steve Simpson, unidentified, Lloyd Taylor, Bill Ruiz, Tim Rivas, and Jeff Ruiz (batboy); (second row) Larry Messmore (coach), Tommy Rivera, Jason Long, unidentified, Jerry Grimm, Armando Gómez, J.D. Simpson, and Jack Jones (manager). Local merchant Bill Ruiz sponsored this team. The store is still in business today on the corner of Lincoln Boulevard and Pacific Street, now being operated by Ruiz's wife, Tillie, and sons Bill Jr. and Jeff. (Courtesy of Tommy Rivera.)

This 1961 Southern League All-Star team consists of, from left to right, (first row) Larry Messmore (coach), Bruce Schoenfilder, Leo Mongrobang, Preston Gilkison, Danny Sáenz, Bill Ruiz, and Jack Jones (manager); (second row) Mike Vásquez, Mike Crapser, Gary Wallace, and Dennis Jones; (third row) Larry Burris, Jason Long, Armando Gómez, Jim Jones, Tommy Rivera, and Lloyd Taylor. This team finished in first place in its district. At St. Monica Catholic High School, Mike Vásquez and Armando Gómez earned All-League honors. (Courtesy of Tommy Rivera.)

In 1961, the Western Boys League Braves team, playing at Los Amigos Park, underwent a uniform change—the Braves uniforms were retired and replaced by Cardinals uniforms. From left to right are (first row) Bobby Félix, unidentified, and Marcie Hernández; (second row) Timmy Rivas, unidentified, Steve Simpson, and Bill Ruiz; (third row) Larry Messmore (coach), two unidentified, Tommy Rivera, Armando Gómez, unidentified, Lloyd Taylor, and Jack Jones (manager). (Courtesy of Tom Rivera.)

This 1962 photograph of 12-year-old Frank Botello was taken at Silva Field in Santa Monica. Silva Field was named after a Mexican coach. Botello's excellent play for the Cubs was rewarded with an All-Star selection in the majors. As an adult, he played five years of men's fast pitch softball on the Bad Company team. Later, he managed his daughters Rebecca and Olivia on a girls' fast pitch travel softball team. His son Frank Jr. played varsity baseball for Culver City High School. In their later years, Botello and his lifelong friends got together quarterly to celebrate their respective birthdays. Since his passing in 2017, his friends are reluctant to continue the tradition. (Courtesy of Frank Botello.)

Many Mexican American players competed at Memorial Park on Fourteenth Street and Olympic Boulevard. This 1962 picture shows brothers Marcie (left) and Bobby Hernández at age 12 and 10 respectively. Coming from an athletic family, they had a remarkable role model in their brother Sal, who was a football hall of famer and played basketball for Santa Monica High School. While at John Adams Jr. High School in 1960, Sal played basketball with former Dodger Rick Monday. In general, when brothers entered the league at the same skill level, they were often placed on the same team for carpool purposes. (Courtesy of Sal Hernández.)

The 1963 Los Amigos All-Star softball team is, from left to right, (first row) ? Hurd, Joe Loporto, Juan Padilla, Pedro Garza, and Rubén Galván; (second row) all unidentified; (third row) unidentified manager, unidentified, Paul Piña, two unidentified, Ricky Vásquez, and unidentified coach. Piña was selected to the All Stars two years older than Little League rules permitted, resulting in the entire team being disqualified. (Courtesy of Pedro Garza.)

The 1966 Santa Monica Pony-Colt Orioles were the defending league champs. From left to right are (first row) Bill Ohland, Pedro Garza, Lawrence Green, Tom Webber, Mike Johnson, and Rodney Sollee; (second row) Bernie Slawter (manager), John Valentini, Duane Espy, Pat McKenna, Kim Anderson, Donald Washington, and Abel Díaz. This team played at John Adams Junior High School in Santa Monica and was sponsored by Byron R. Woodley's Shell station. Pedro Garza played baseball and Abel Díaz played football at Santa Monica High School. (Courtesy of Pedro Garza.)

Marine Park in Santa Monica hosted an independent baseball league in 1966. From left to right are (first row) Tommy Sánchez, unidentified, Gilbert Carranza, Tony Macneil, and Johnny Soto (manager); (second row) Bob Klein, unidentified, Rupert Casillas, Ray Romo, and Joe Esparza. In 1971, Esparza lost his life in the Vietnam War. His name is engraved on a memorial wall at Santa Monica's Woodlawn Cemetery. (Courtesy of Ray Romo.)

Santa Monica High School won the 4A California Interscholastic Federation (CIF) championship in 1973 at Dodger Stadium. From left to right are (first row) Billy McDonald, Ralph Morphy, Mike Rains, Bruce Walkup, and Jeff Eppling; (second row) John Espy, Raúl Sáenz, Steve Vollmer, Cliffton Smith, Jim Gilchrist, and Terry Bevington; (third row) Byron McLaughlin, Alan Gleisner, Ainslie Washington, Dave Wisebart, John Eichenhauer, and Anthony Williams. Sáenz was the only Mexican American on the team. (Courtesy of Raúl Sáenz.)

Tomás Rivera coached Pony League at John Adams Junior High School and Colt League at Marine Park, both in Santa Monica. After his coaching days, he became an umpire for the Southern California Umpires Association, from the early 1970s into the 1980s. He was known to use the phrase, "You are out, son" whenever a batter struck out. Always impartial, he once called his grandson Brian out looking on the third strike while umpiring his game. Rivera is pictured here in his umpire uniform with granddaughter Mónica Varela. (Courtesy of Tommy Rivera.)

SO. CALIF. UMPIRES ASSN.

3 2

SOUTHERN CALIFORNIA UMPIRES ASSOCIATION

ACTIVE MEMBER

TOM RIVERA

10/31/80 William J Pulfer

This Card Expires Treasurer

The umpire ID card for Tomás Rivera indicated that he had completed his annual umpire recertification with the Southern California Umpires Association. Rivera primarily umpired on the Westside. Many Mexican Americans chose to continue their participation as umpires, scorekeepers, and statisticians upon hanging up their cleats. (Courtesy of Tommy Rivera.)

Frank Cásarez, a 1975 Santa Monica High School graduate, was a right-handed varsity pitcher and second baseman. Immediately after high school, he played for the San Diego State University Aztecas. He was recruited by the Mexican team Los Tigres (The Tigers). In 1980, he played single A for the Clinton Giants and Fresno Giants, the farm teams of the San Francisco Giants. He also played for the Astros, an independent league farm team in Northern California. Cásarez was their pitching ace, leading the team in wins, strikeouts, and earned run average. (Courtesy of Frank Cásarez.)

Fabiola González grew up in Santa Monica in the 1970s in a one-bedroom apartment with her mom and three brothers. Her mother worked two jobs. González developed her skills playing Santa Monica Bobby Sox softball in the sixth grade. At Santa Monica High School, she excelled as a softball player. (Courtesy of Fabiola González.)

This photograph was taken during the first no-hitter Fabiola González pitched while at Santa Monica High School in 1994 as a freshman. As a sophomore, in the first game of a double header, she had a single, a triple, a home run, and four runs batted in. In the second game, this all-around player pitched her second no-hitter. In 1997, in a marathon Bay League softball match, she pitched 22 innings, the equivalent of three games, in an event that lasted five hours and fifteen minutes. (Courtesy of Fabiola González.)

At Santa Monica High School, as a freshman, Fabiola González was honored for pitching the winning game for a fourth consecutive Bay League title in 1994. That same season, she was listed as a Top 10 Female Athlete. In 1995, The *Los Angeles Times* and the *Santa Monica Evening Outlook* selected her as the Player of the Year and First Team pitcher/shortstop. She led her team in home runs and was selected to the All Westside softball team, and was named First Team by the Bay League Softball Association. Her baseball career ended after high school. Today, more girls are recruited by colleges to play softball. (Courtesy of Fabiola González.)

The *Santa Monica Evening Outlook* named Fabiola González to the First Team All-Westside Softball Team in 1994. She garnered many awards in high school, including All-CIF, Outlook Player of the Year, Number-Two Top Female Athlete of the Year, First Team by the Southern Section Softball Association, All-Westside Honor for all four seasons, and the team's Most Valuable Player twice. She was voted the Most Athletic in 1997. In 1998, González was selected to the All-Conference Softball Team at El Camino College. (Courtesy of Fabiola González.)

From left to right are brothers Raymond, Rudy, and Sammy Romo. Seven Romo brothers (Sammy, Ralph, Raoul, Louis, Joe, Rudy, and David), and three Romo nephews (Raymond, Ralph, and Samuel Jr.) played men's league softball on the same team in the late 1970s. The team captain presented the lineup to the plate umpire listing all positions and the batting order simply as "Romo." The umpire insisted on seeing this "superman" who could simultaneously play all positions. As each batter approached the plate, the fans whooped and hollered as the name Romo was announced. (Courtesy of Ray Romo.)

At St. Monica's High School in Santa Monica, Ben Agatep played third base for the Mariners. He began to be scouted in his Junior year (2000–2001) by colleges and Major League Baseball teams. He felt this was the year when his physical ability was starting to meet his mental ability. He was selected to the All-League first team by the Camino Real League, won All-CIF honors his senior year, and earned All-League each season he played. (Courtesy of Ben Agatep.)

Ben Agatep played for the San Jose State Spartans in 2002 before suffering a season-ending knee injury. His remarkable perseverance and determination enabled him to return to the game he loved. His team competed against the University of Southern California, California State University at Long Beach and at Fullerton, and Stanford. (Courtesy of Ben Agatep.)

Culver City

Culver City is an independent municipality on the west side of Los Angeles, five and a half miles from the coast. The Tongva-Gabrielino Indians were the original inhabitants, settling along the creek named La Ballona. By 1822, under Mexican rule, brothers Augustin and Ygnacio Machado and cousins Felipe and Tomás Talamantes founded Rancho La Ballona, bringing relief to many Mexican families escaping the inland heat of el Pueblo de Los Angeles. Another prominent Mexican family, the Sáenz family, opened the first dry goods store in Culver City. The Figueroa family donated land to build the first church, St. Augustine, completed in 1887, and the Lugo family established the Lugo Ranch when Mercurial Lugo married Rita Reyes. Harry Culver filed Main Street, the original street of Culver City, at the Los Angeles Recorder's Office in 1913. Culver City was incorporated on September 20, 1917, and adopted the motto "The Heart of Screenland," as the Thomas Ince movie studio merged with Metro Goldwyn Mayer, home of *The Wizard of Oz*.

A mix of old and new businesses made Culver City unique: Western Stove started the industry boom in 1922, followed by Steller and Skoog Hardware, Beacon Laundry, National Guard Armory, and Howard Hughes Aircraft. Major automobile dealerships opened along Washington Boulevard, the Culver City Kennel Club was granted a permit for dog racing, and Speedway Corporation constructed an auto race course. Helms Bakery, established in 1932, delivered fresh bread and donuts daily throughout Westside and Los Angeles in the world-famous Helms Bakery trucks. For decades, the historical López Ranch provided fresh fruit and vegetables to Westside families, and a pumpkin patch and Christmas tree lot brought joy to children during the holidays. Culver City families found year-round entertainment at the Studio Drive-In Theater, the Roller Dome, and Culver City Ice Rink. Service organizations such as the American Legion, AMVETS, Lions Club, Elks Lodge, Exchange Club, and Rotary Club of Culver City became important parts of the local community. Veteran's Memorial Park, home to Fiesta La Ballona, founded in 1951, celebrates local Mexican heritage every August, showcasing community diversity during the three-day neighborhood event.

In the early 1950s, with the construction of Veteran's Memorial Park and Culver City High School, sports became an important part of the neighborhood. Veteran's Memorial Park housed the Culver Plunge and softball diamonds; Culver City High School housed the baseball field and Helm's Field for football and track. Culver American Little League established fields near La Ballona Wetlands, and Culver National Little League teams played at Ron Smith Field. Culver City has produced outstanding teams, players, and coaches, with Mexican Americans contributing greatly. This chapter highlights their successful accomplishments and stories.

In 1959, the Prieto brothers were ready to play ball as toddlers. Their father, Antonio V. Prieto, emigrated from Michoacan. He had them watch players like Willie McCovey, Willie Mays, and the Alou brothers. They played pickup games with the Reyes, Moraga, and Márquez families and organized Little League at Culver American with the Camacho brothers, Joe Valdez, and Gilbert Ortega. The Prietos formed the Giants softball team at Veteran's Memorial Park and were an all-brother infield: Rick at first, Bobby at second, Mario at shortstop, and Tony at third. From left to right are Bobby, Rick, Mario, and Tony. (Courtesy of Antonio V. Prieto.)

The 1979 Culver American champion Athletics were sponsored by the Culver City firefighters. From left to right are (first row) Christina Moreno, unidentified, David Sánchez, Kim Morgan, Gerard Van Gerwen, and unidentified; (second row) Marcel Van Gerwen (coach), James Banks, Ray Sánchez, unidentified, Lori Moreno (team mom), David López, unidentified, and Jesse Sánchez (coach). Coach Sánchez was proud to have two girls contributing their good fielding and hitting to this team, giving it the chemistry needed for a great season. (Courtesy of Jesse Sánchez.)

In 1974, team captain Rick Prieto led his team in hitting and fielded first base for the Culver City High School (CCHS) Centaurs under head coach Dave Ruebsamen. He became head baseball coach at CCHS in 1994. Today, he demonstrates his mastery of hitting to his players and his travel team, the Culver City Orioles. In 2003, he was inducted into CCHS's Athletic Hall of Fame as a three-sport athlete in baseball, football, and wrestling. (Courtesy of James Ruebsamen, ©1974.)

The 1974 CCHS Centaurs placed second in the Ocean League, advancing to the first round of the CIF Division 3 playoffs, losing to Cabrillo High School. From left to right are (first row) Glen Hotchkin, Richard Hiskey, Rick Prieto, Ernie Sáenz, Barry Helfend, Dave Girón, Mike Lambert, and Rodney Benson; (second row) Mark Brooks, Steve Benson, Mario Robles, John Romero, Bill Goodwin, Bob Cervi, Chuck Menzhuber, and Dave Ruebsamen (head coach). (Courtesy of James Ruebsamen, ©1974.)

January 9, 1975

Mr. John A. Romero
5457 Kingston Avenue
Culver City, CA 90230

Dear John:

Congratulations! You have been selected by the Detroit Organization in the Regular Free Agent Draft.

An authorized representative of the Detroit Tigers will contact you.

Sincerely,

Bill Lajoie

Bill Lajoie
Director of Scouting

BL/gsk

John Romero (third row, fifth from left), an infielder from Culver City High School, was drafted by the Detroit Tigers in 1975. His first team was in Bristol, Tennessee, in the Appalachian League. He then played with the Lakeland Tigers in the Florida State League under manager Jim Leyland. Romero played minor-league baseball with outstanding teammates such as Alan Trammell (2018 Baseball Hall of Fame inductee), Lou Whitaker, and Dan Petry. (Courtesy of John Romero.)

Los Angeles–born John Romero moved to Culver City with his family at age eight. He started playing baseball at Ron Smith Field, continuing through high school. He graduated from CCHS in 1974 and played shortstop for the Santa Monica City College Corsairs. Pictured is his signing letter from the Detroit Tigers. He played in the organization for three years. Romero has worked for American Airlines for 40 years. He married his wife, Liz, in 1996 and resides in Southern California with their daughter Jayne. (Courtesy of John Romero.)

Rick Prieto signed his first professional contract with the Rojos de Caborca in the Liga Norte de Sonora in 1981. He was known as Ricardo and was coached by Kiko Castro. Fernando Valenzuela graciously posed for a picture while visiting his brother, Prieto's teammate. When Prieto played for the Algodoneros de Guasave and Diablos Rojos del México, his travels spanned from Tijuana to the Yucatan Peninsula. His native Mexican teammates included Alfonso Pulido, Houston Jiménez, Teddy Higuera, and Mario Mendoza, who all played in Major League Baseball. Prieto is grateful for all the opportunities and friendships he enjoyed while playing the game of baseball. (Courtesy of Rick Prieto.)

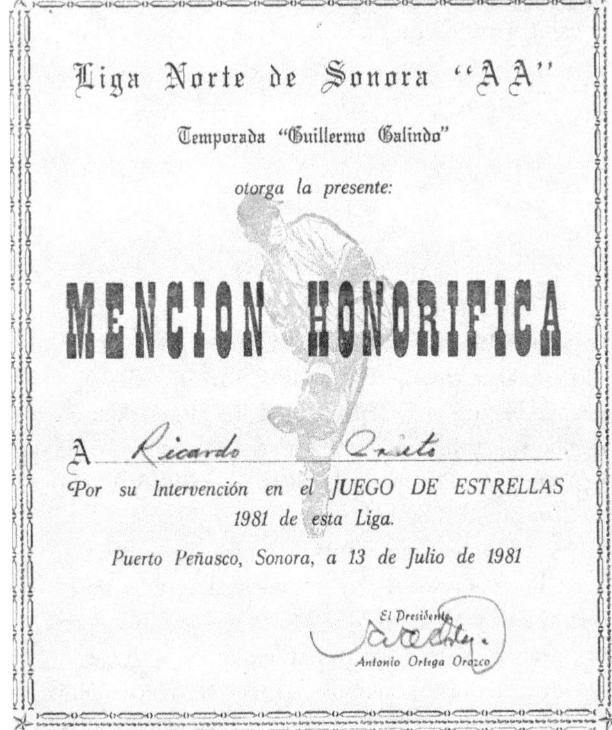

Liga Norte de Sonora "AA"

Temporada "Guillermo Galindo"

otorga la presente:

MENCION HONORIFICA

A Ricardo Prieto

Por su Intervención en el JUEGO DE ESTRELLAS 1981 de esta Liga.

Puerto Peñasco, Sonora, a 13 de Julio de 1981

El Presidente

Antonio Ortega Orozco

Lefty Rick Prieto was a natural hitter. He garnered All-Conference honors at Santa Monica City College and Arizona Western, earning a scholarship to the University of San Diego. He played on the Santa Monica Collegiate team with Pete O'Brien (MLB), Tim Oliveraz, and John Violette (MLB), and earned the California Collegiate League batting title. With the Rojos de Caborca, he earned the batting title and set the record for doubles in the Sonora League. Prieto was managed by American League batting champion Tony Oliva while playing in the Mexican Pacific Coast League. His teammates included Scott Ullger, Randy Bush, and Kevin Bass. (Courtesy of Rick Prieto.)

Rick Prieto from Culver City (left) and Víctor Prieto from San Pedro met in 1981 while playing for the Rojos de Caborca. In 1982, their contracts were purchased by rival teams; Rick went to the Diablos Rojos del México and Víctor to the Tigres del México. They were reunited when Víctor was traded to the Diablos mid-season. They enjoyed their experience with Mexican American teammates Ernie Camacho (MLB), Ramón Murillo, and Bobby Rodríguez. One of Rick's highlights with the Diablos Rojos was executing a game-winning hit off of Luís Tiant (Boston Red Sox). (Courtesy of Rick Prieto.)

Jesse Plasencia Jr., born to Jesse and Virginia Plasencia in Santa Monica, was raised in Culver City. He played Little League at Culver American, earning All–Ocean League Honors at CCHS. In 1978, he played American Legion baseball, contributing to the championship game in Yountville. Plasencia played at West Los Angeles College and Cal State Los Angeles. In 1982–1983, he played for the San Francisco Giants scout team. Mike Brito of the LA Dodgers noticed his talent as a southpaw with an awesome screwball reminiscent of Fernando Valenzuela. When he signed with the Dodgers, he was issued No. 43, the reverse jersey number of Valenzuela, No. 34. (Courtesy of Jesse Plasencia Jr.)

Jesse Plasencia Jr.'s dream of becoming a Los Angeles Dodger was not fulfilled when a last minute signee replaced him. However, Mike Brito believed in his talent and orchestrated a contract for him to play in México with the Soles de San Luis. Pictured is his contract, showing the particulars such as salary, room, and board. Playing for the Soles was instrumental in furthering Plasencia's career in México. In 1983, he played a game in Ensenada, Baja California, and struck out the Mexican league batting champ twice to get the attention of the Leones scouts. Again, Mike Brito aided in the contract process and Plasencia became a *beisbolista* for the Leones de Yucatan. Other Culver City players throughout the years have received international contracts to play in México and Colombia. (Courtesy of Jesse Plasencia Jr.)

CLUB DE BEISBOL PROFESIONAL
SOLES DE SAN LUIS
Av. Juarez y 6ta. Altos Tel. 4-27-37 — Tel. Particular 4-19-06
San Luis Rio Colorado, Sonora

San Luis Rio Colorado Son., Junio 13 de 1983.

A QUIEN CORRESPONDA:

El Club de Beisbol Profesional de San Luis que participa dentro de la Liga Norte de Sonora, Clase -"AA" Con esta Fecha Firmará para que juegue Beisbol Profesional dentro de nuestro Club, el Sr. JESUS PLACENSIA.

Por lo antes Expuesto solicitamos atentamente las facilidades necesarias para que pueda firmar -el Contrato con nuestro Club , Dicho jugador obtendra un-Sueldo de $ 48,000.00 M.N. Mensuales y gastos de Hospedaje y alimentos cuando nuestro Equipo este de Gira, los gastos que origine en casa seran cubiertos por el Propio Jugador.

A T E N T A M E N T E
CLUB DE BEISBOL PROFESIONAL
"SOLES"

GONZALO DE LA VEGA — Presidente
EMIGDIO VILLAESCUSA S. — Gerente.

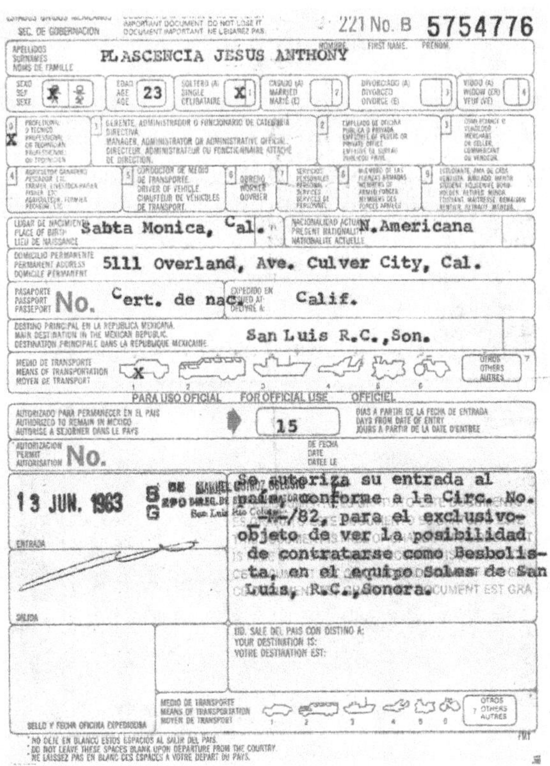

SEC. DE GOBERNACION — IMPORTANT DOCUMENT DO NOT LOSE IT — DOCUMENT IMPORTANT NE L'EGAREZ PAS — 221 No. B 5754776

APELLIDOS / SURNAMES / NOMS DE FAMILLE — NOMBRE / FIRST NAME / PRENOM: PLASCENCIA JESUS ANTHONY

SEXO / SEX / SEXE: X — EDAD / AGE / AGE: 23 — SOLTERO (A) / SINGLE / CELIBATAIRE: X

0 PROFESIONAL O TECNICO / PROFESSIONAL OR TECHNICIAN: X

LUGAR DE NACIMIENTO / PLACE OF BIRTH / LIEU DE NAISSANCE: Sabta Monica, Cal.
NACIONALIDAD ACTUAL / PRESENT NATIONALITY / NATIONALITE ACTUELLE: N. Americana

DOMICILIO PERMANENTE / PERMANENT ADDRESS / DOMICILE PERMANENT: 5111 Overland, Ave. Culver City, Cal.

PASAPORTE / PASSPORT / PASSEPORT No. Cert. de nac. — EXPEDIDO EN / ISSUED AT / DELIVRE A: Calif.

DESTINO PRINCIPAL EN LA REPUBLICA MEXICANA / MAIN DESTINATION IN THE MEXICAN REPUBLIC / DESTINATION PRINCIPALE DANS LA REPUBLIQUE MEXICAINE: San Luis R.C., Son.

MEDIO DE TRANSPORTE / MEANS OF TRANSPORTATION / MOYEN DE TRANSPORT: 1 X

PARA USO OFICIAL — FOR OFFICIAL USE — OFFICIEL

AUTORIZADO PARA PERMANECER EN EL PAIS / AUTHORIZED TO REMAIN IN MEXICO / AUTORISE A SEJOURNER DANS LE PAYS: 15 DIAS A PARTIR DE LA FECHA DE ENTRADA / DAYS FROM DATE OF ENTRY / JOURS A PARTIR DE LA DATE D'ENTREE

AUTORIZACION / PERMIT / AUTORISATION No. — DE FECHA / DATE / DATEE LE

13 JUN. 1983 — ENTRADA

Se autoriza su entrada al país, conforme a la Circ. No. -M-/82, para el exclusivo objeto de ver la posibilidad de contratarse como Besbolista, en el equipo Soles de San Luis, R.C., Sonora.

SALIDA

UD. SALE DEL PAIS CON DISTINO A: / YOUR DESTINATION IS: / VOTRE DESTINATION EST:

SELLO Y FECHA OFICINA EXPEDIDORA — MEDIO DE TRANSPORTE / MEANS OF TRANSPORTATION / MOYEN DE TRANSPORT

NO DEJE EN BLANCO ESTOS ESPACIOS AL SALIR DEL PAIS. / DO NOT LEAVE THESE SPACES BLANK UPON DEPARTURE FROM THE COUNTRY. / NE LAISSEZ PAS EN BLANC CES ESPACES A VOTRE DEPART DU PAYS.

Seen here is the international work permit for Jesse Plasencia Jr. This document is required by all foreign born nationals working in México. In this case, Plasencia, who applied for the work permit as a beisbolista, was called a *pocho*, as were all the other Mexican Americans who played baseball in México. During border checks throughout México, the pochos were careful not to disclose they were beisbolistas from the United States, as it was costly to do so. One highlight was when Plasencia played for the Leones in the 1985 division championship game as defending champs, but lost the bid to repeat. He pitched before a crowd of 43,000. His career in México spanned three years, traveling to almost every part of the country. (Courtesy of Jesse Plasencia Jr.)

Jesse Plasencia Jr. (right) signed with the Leones de Yucatan in 1985. Pictured in the bullpen area of Parque Kukulcán with roommate Juan Rincón from Pico Rivera, California, Plasencia received the full major-league experience: children of all ages adoring him and asking him for his autograph in pure awe of this star pitcher. He was managed by legendary Mexican League coach Carlos Paz, who also had him play for him in the Pacific Coast League with the Delfines (Dolphins) de Puerto Vallarta. After a truly memorable experience, Plasencia returned to his hometown and coached at Culver City High School and at Santa Monica Police Activity League from 1990 to 1996. He now lives in the South Bay Area with his wife, Lorie, and still enjoys the good ol' game of baseball. (Courtesy of Jesse Plasencia Jr.)

The newly established 1983 Major Softball All Stars played their games at Culver American field. From left to right are (first row) Tiffany Glostner and Denise Sánchez; (second row) Natalie García, Paola ?, Valerie Hernández, Linda Olivera, Nanette Armendérez, and Lisa Purnell; (third row) Sue Atencio (team mom), Eloisa Miranda, Patty Palka, Ginger Atencio, Ilona Sánchez (coach), Nancy Del Santos, Julianna Darkins, and Natalie Dennis Valenzuela (coach). Coach Jesse Sánchez is not pictured. This team won Little League District 25 and Section 5 championships, comprised of players from the Lady Bugs, Slick Chicks, and Liberty Belles. (Courtesy of Jesse Sánchez.)

The 1984 Culver City American Senior Baseball All Stars won the District 25 and Section 5 championships. From left to right are (first row) Roger Serafín, Tony Bañuelos, Don "Chico" García, Roland Villaseñor, Michael Mestas, Vince Rivera, and Darrin Okimoto; (second row) R.J. Mestas (coach), Mike Bates, Bobby Velásquez, Adolfo Leones, John Camacho, Ricardo Valquez, Jesse Sánchez (coach), and David Andrus. This team reached the regionals but lost in the second round. Many of the Latino players had successful high school and college careers. (Courtesy of Jesse Sánchez.)

Yvonne Gutíerrez, one of a set of triplets, was born and raised in Culver City with her two brothers. The softball player at CCHS was twice named the Most Valuable Player in the Ocean League and All-CIF Southern Section player. She attended UCLA, playing softball as an outfielder and top hitter from 1989 to 1992. She played on three NCAA championship squads, earning first-team All-America honors and winning the triple crown her senior year. She was named to the Women's College World Series All-Tournament Team three times, was a four-time All-Pac-10 honoree, and in 2013 was inducted into the UCLA Hall of Fame. Gutíerrez is an engineer with the Los Angeles City Fire Department and resides on the Westside. (Courtesy of Yvonne Gutíerrez.)

The 1999 Ocean League champion Culver City High School advanced to the second round of the CIF playoffs. From left to right are (first row) Sean Smith, David Leos, Nigel Martín, Paul Díaz, Gabriel Cancino, and Lehnman Johnson; (second row) Joel Mitchell, Nick Nagy, Scott Sachen, Tony Walsh, Devaughn Wallace, Jacob (Botello) Levy, Vince Cueva, Luís Aceves, and Eric Allen; (third row) Walter Holland, Sean Bergmans, Ron Ozaki (coach), Jaime Miranda (coach), Rick Prieto (head coach), Ben Dudley (coach), Jarvis Redwine (coach), Héctor Zamora, and Phillip Veals. This team won with determination, competiveness, and winning attitudes. (Courtesy of Rick Prieto.)

Since the late 1950s, the CCHS baseball program dressed in the football locker room. Around 1990–1991, Jerry Chabola (head coach) decided the program needed its own locker room. An old Army Quonset hut was divided into three sections: front for storage and varsity lockers, middle for lower-level lockers, and back for a coaches' office. The "Hut" for the Mighty Centaurs became an iconic sanctuary for almost 10 years under Chabola's successor Rick Prieto. It was demolished in early 2000 and replaced by a mobile classroom, the "Clubhouse." (Courtesy of Rick Prieto.)

Héctor Zamora, born in Westwood and raised in Culver City, was an active scholar-athlete at CCHS, participating in baseball, soccer, and football. He was also involved with the Associated Student Body and Latinos Unidos. He was named First Team All–Ocean League (1997–1999); First Team All-CIF (1999); Ocean League MVP as a senior pitcher; Westside All-Star Game MVP (1999); and *Daily Breeze* Player of the Year (1999). He attended Cerritos Community College, where he was a two-year member of the South Coast Conference baseball team. Zamora earned a full scholarship to San Jose State and was named First Team All–Western Athletic Conference while studying business management. (Courtesy Héctor Zamora.)

In 2002, Héctor Zamora was drafted by the New York Yankees, and played in the organization for three and a half years. He was voted Fan Favorite twice and was once the team's MVP. Zamora also played in Colombia and México. He earned his bachelor of arts from San Jose State and the University of Phoenix, and master of science from Azusa Pacific University in physical education. He was an assistant coach for 11 years combined at West Los Angeles and Cerritos Community Colleges. In June 2018, he was named head baseball coach of the Cerritos Community College Falcons. He resides in Culver City with his wife, Sherry, and son Zander. (Courtesy of Héctor Zamora.)

The American Legion Community Post 46 in Culver City opened its doors in April 1967. It sponsored American Legion and Little League teams and hosted youth sports banquets. This is one of many CCHS baseball program banquets held at Post 46. Sandra Prieto (first row, center) played Little League softball at Westchester's Nielsen Park. CCHS assistant baseball coaches pictured are, from left to right, William (Gonzáles) Minguet, Ron Ozaki, Jaime Miranda, and head coach Rick Prieto. The post had many Mexican American veterans as members, including several who served as post commander. (Courtesy of Rebecca García-Prieto.)

Roger (Aviña) Packard Jr. was born and raised in Culver City. He played for Culver City National Little League (CCNLL) at Ron Smith Field from 1980 to 1985. At the age of 12, he was the home run champ of record at the original CCNLL and member of the 1985 All-Star team. He played on the 15-year-old Babe Ruth state championship team, becoming the Pacific Western Regional representatives in Oahu, Hawaii. Packard played for CCHS and was on the varsity Ocean League championship teams in 1989 and 1990. In his senior year, he garnered All–Ocean League First Team honors and was an All-Star game participant. (Courtesy of Roger [Aviña] Packard Jr.)

The 1986 Culver City Babe Ruth Major A's league champions were, from left to right, (first row) John Grillet, Steve Molina, Alex Bravo, Juan Cueva, Rámon Veral, Adam White, Mario Fragoso, and Roger (Aviña) Packard Jr.; (second row) Joe Sáenz (coach), Jose Estavil Sr. (coach), Albaro Ibarra, Dan Melendez, Ariel Martín, Jose Estavil Jr., Mauricio Estavil, Mary Melendez (team mom), and Carlos Melendez (coach). Several Latino teammates were selected for the All Star team that won district, state, and regional championships, and placed fourth in the Babe Ruth World Series. Some had successful high school, college, and pro careers. (Courtesy of Roger [Aviña] Packard Jr.)

Competitive men's leagues found a home at Culver City High School's baseball field. The players say it is the best field on the Westside. Many Latino players grew up attending Westside high schools where baseball camaraderie is a way of life, bringing their families to enjoy Sunday games for decades. From left to right are (first row) William (Gonzáles) Minguet, Jake Alba, Brian Monreal, Jaime Miranda, Ray Wilson, and Dave Valdez; (second row) Eric Arue, Mark Farner, Shay López, Martin Campbell, Steve Benson, Dion Deas, Rick Prieto, and Rob Kivo. (Courtesy of Jaime Miranda.)

Juan Cueva was born in Los Angeles and raised in Culver City as the oldest of six siblings. He played Little League baseball from the age of six through Babe Ruth League at Culver City's Ron Smith Field. At Culver City High School, he earned all-league honors. Cueva graduated from CCHS in 1989, going on to earn his bachelor of arts and master of science degrees in behavioral science from Cal State–Dominguez Hills. He was named head coach for West Torrance High School in 2001. His honors include four-time Bay League Coach of the Year; CIF semifinalist in 2006; and the Pioneer League championship in 2016. (Courtesy of Juan Cueva.)

The 2006 Culver City High School Centaur softball team advanced to the first round of the CIF playoffs, losing to California High School in Whittier. From left to right are (first row) Chelsey Kinnon, Lindsey Eichenberger, Jackie Gallarza, and Portia Boddicker; (second row) Jazmin Velásquez, Gabriela Chávez, Brenda López, and Crystal Murillo; (third row) Sarah Drust, Willie Eichenberger (coach), John Sargeant (head coach), Duane Briggs (coach), and Jasmin Zamudio; (fourth row) Tatiana Motuapuaka, Sandra Prieto, Christina Schlothauer, and Kaleigh Grinley. (Courtesy of Sandra Prieto.)

Members of the 2001 junior varsity CCHS Centaur softball team pose for a picture. From left to right are (first row) Michelle García, Ana Sybille, and Lourdes Escobar; (second row) Ashley Stewart and Jessi Serra; (third row) Ray Serra Jr. (coach), Jessica Corona, and Traci Carr (team manager). For decades, the softball program practiced and played at Veteran's Memorial Park (Vet's Park). In 2000, a softball field was constructed on CCHS's multipurpose field, and the varsity team moved there. The junior varsity and freshman/sophomore teams remained at Vet's Park. (Courtesy of Jessica Corona.)

The 2006 Culver City High School Centaurs had an awesome season. A five-game Lion's Club tournament win in San Diego started a 13-game winning streak and Ocean League title. From left to right are (first row) Jaime Miranda (coach), Andrew Connolly, Percy Pérez, Anthony Rincón, Daniel Reyes, Kevin Ozaki, Fernando Hernández Ruiz, James Smith, and Ben Dudley (coach); (second row) Rick Prieto (head coach), MaCarrin Tucker, Jeremy Burrell, Kevin Cohen, David Smith, Jose Tostado, Adrian Campos, Jacob Blodgett, Jack Maeshiro, Ryan Sherriff, Matt Mercier, and Jimmy Seay. (Courtesy of the Burrell family.)

From left to right are Ramón García, Rick Prieto, Sandra Prieto, Rebecca García-Prieto, and Hilda García. Rámon and Hilda were born and raised in Santa Monica. When Rámon returned from the Marine Corps, he married Hilda in 1957. They purchased their Culver City home in 1966 and raised their daughters and grandchildren there. Rámon and Hilda became baseball fans when Rick married Rebecca and baseball became a way of life. In 2018, Ramón passed away at age 86. (Courtesy of Rebecca García-Prieto.)

The 2010 CCHS Centaurs won the Ocean League championship under head coach Rick Prieto and advanced to the second round of the CIF playoffs. From left to right are (first row) Lenard Méndez, Michael Lee, George Aceves Jr., and Adrian Pérez; (second row) Alejandro Andrews, Rodney Bradley, Sean Cogman, Daniel Byun, Dylan Soules, Lukas O'Conner, Ryan Mulvihill, Tyler Mark, Garrett Gemgnani, Jon Kocker, Tyler Adkinson, and Devin Sylvester. (Courtesy of George Lasse.)

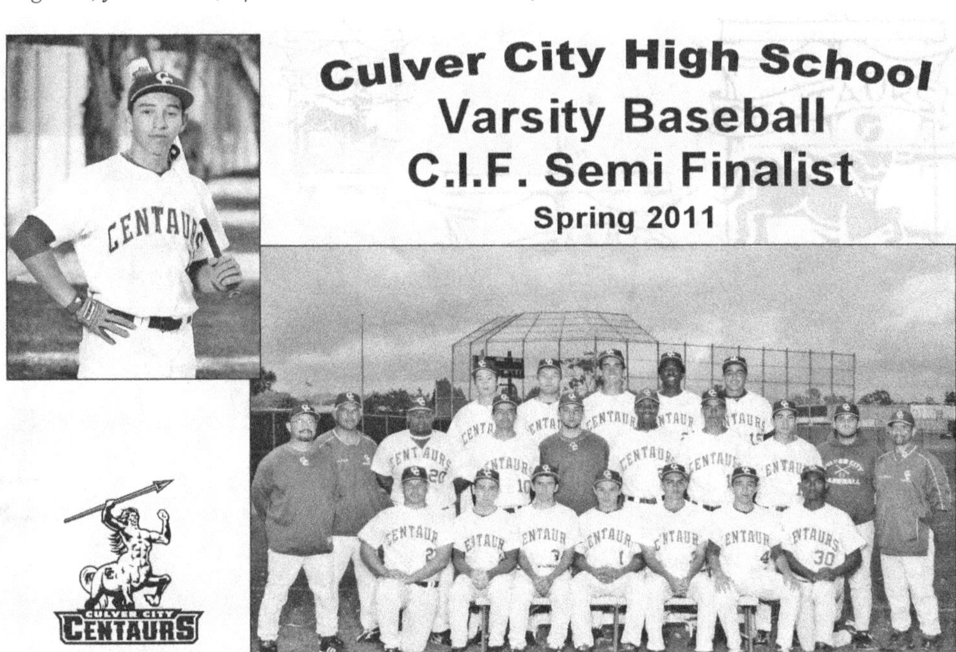

Coach Prieto's Centaurs advanced to the CIF Division 3 semifinal game in 2011 for the second time in school history. Hundreds of fans cheered them on, but it was a heartbreaking loss at home against Woodbridge, 2-1. The featured player in the top left corner, team captain George Aceves Jr., also played on the undefeated 2012 Ocean League championship team. While attending Loyola Marymount University, Aceves coached the CCHS freshman/sophomore baseball team, majored in business entrepreneurship, was a member of club baseball, as well as president of the business fraternity Delta Sigma Pi. (Courtesy of Diana Aceves, CFP Studio Photography.)

The District 25 Little League Challengers program is for kids with special needs, and home field is at Culver City High School. For over 10 years, Jesse Sánchez (retired District 25 Little League umpire in chief) has been the administrator and umpire for these teams. (Courtesy of Jesse Sánchez.)

The undefeated 2016 Ocean League champs from Culver City High School are, from left to right, (first row) Ryan Weiner, Rick Prieto (head coach), and Tomás Saucedo; (second row) Joseph Pérez, Jason Zeidman, Matthew Paspalis, Kelvin Murillo, and Mason Mulvihill; (third row) Daniel Aceves, Eli Saucedo, Hunter Hutchinson, Michael Netzel, Max Sterner, Nolan Martínez, Matthew Rummelsburg, Jacob Weiner, and Justin Weiner. Rick Prieto was honored as Ocean League Coach of the Year for the fifth time. Most of this team had played together since Little League. (Courtesy of Rick Prieto.)

Venice, West Los Angeles, and Westwood

Venice is a residential, commercial, and recreational beachfront neighborhood within Los Angeles. It is located within the urban region of western Los Angeles County known as the Westside.

Venice was founded in 1905 as a seaside resort town. It was an independent city until 1926, when it merged with Los Angeles. Venice is bounded on the northwest by the Santa Monica city line, on the northeast by Mar Vista, on the southeast by Culver City, Del Rey, and Marina Del Rey, on the south by Ballona Creek, and on the west by the Pacific Ocean.

Los Angeles had neglected Venice so long that, by the 1950s, it had become the "Slum by the Sea." Low rents for rundown bungalows attracted many Mexican migrants. By 2002, the numbers of people of color in Venice were reduced due to gentrification. Today, Venice is known for its canals, beaches, and the circus-like Ocean Front Walk, a two-and-a-half-mile pedestrian promenade that features performers, mystics, artists, vendors, and many homeless.

West Los Angeles is a residential and commercial neighborhood in the city of Los Angeles. The neighborhood is divided by the Interstate 405 freeway. Santa Monica borders the west, Culver City the south. The Westside region is partially comprised of Ladera Heights, Mar Vista, Palms, Sawtelle, and Westwood.

In the 2000 census, the Westside (as defined by the *Los Angeles Times*) had a population of 529,427. In 2000, non-Hispanic whites made up 63 percent of the population.

The Westside is home to the University of California, Los Angeles (UCLA), a public research university in the Westwood neighborhood. It is the second-oldest of the 10 campuses of the University of California system. Notable Latinos who have attended UCLA are Juan Felipe Herrera (US poet laureate), Héctor Ambriz (baseball), Efren Herrera (football), David Estrada (soccer), Nicholas Paul Rimando (soccer), Lisa Fernández (softball), Antonio Villaraigosa (politics), Carlos Castañeda (writer/anthropologist) and Dan Guerrero (baseball and athletics).

Frank Redondo's love for baseball is second to none. He played baseball at every opportunity on any team that would have him. He started playing seriously at Venice High School, where he was on the varsity team. Upon graduation, he continued to play in independent leagues. Later, he began to play men's B softball with the Truckers. As the years passed, Redondo played on many teams, culminating with an Indian reservation league. This 1977 picture of Redondo was taken in Palmdale, California, during tournament play. His daughter Selena played varsity softball at Culver City High School and was named First Team in the Ocean League. (Courtesy of Vince García Sr.)

From Venice, John Huerta played organized baseball since he was nine years old. A gifted player, he could play any position. Huerta played varsity baseball at Venice High School in the early 1970s, earning All–Western League Honors as a senior. As an adult, he played men's softball B league with many local teams, including the Indians and Bad Company. Following in his footsteps, his daughter Angela was selected Girls Junior All-Star for North Venice Little League. In 2002, she had the honor of playing in the Little League World Series for girls. (Courtesy of Vince García Sr.)

Joey Carrillo is pictured at a tournament in 1981. He played varsity baseball for Venice High School in the mid 1970s. Upon graduation, he was sought after by many B-level local fastpitch men's teams, including the Truckers and the Amazements, with whom he played. Carrillo coached Girls Junior All Stars at North Venice Little League. In 2002, this team, which included his daughter Candice, competed in the Little League World Series for girls in Kirkland, Washington, but did not win. Since 2003, Carrillo has coached the girls' varsity team at St. Monica Catholic High School. (Courtesy of Vince García Sr.)

This 1982 We Bad softball team includes nine family members. From left to right are (first row) unidentified, Ray Serra Jr., Richard Casarez, Ron Sánchez, and Rene Echerribal; (second row) Charlie Martínez, Don Reyes, Joe Sandoval, Steve Dudley, Manuel Ybarra, and Mike Rivera. Prior to officially organizing in league play, these family members organized games during Sunday get-togethers. Upon realizing the talents within the group, they joined league play. This Venice team played on the senior field at Culver American for four seasons. (Courtesy of Mike Rivera.)

Several Venice residents played on the 1977 Graders softball team. From left to right are (first row) Marino Molina, Vince García Jr., Sammy Romo Jr., Ray Romo, and Joey García; (second row) Vince García Sr., Gilbert Sandoval, Stan Busman, Rudy Romo, Greg Losman, John Huerta, and Chris Cruz. (Courtesy of Vince García Sr.)

The Westside Indians included players from several area high schools, including Inglewood, Venice, University, St. Monica Catholic, Santa Monica, Culver City, Beverly Hills, and Hamilton. From left to right are (first row) David Barajas, Rubén Camacho, Isaac Yoshinaga, Eric Alcalá, Derek Moore, Brad Winklejohn, Eddie Morales, Matt Levy, and Dennis Hightower; (second row) Mike McCaffery, Sheldon Phillip Guide, Lonnie Jackson, Gino McGowens, Reid Algian, unidentified, Jamie Carrillo, Víctor Alcalá, Ricardo Zamorano, and Bobby Dobson. The boy in front, directly behind the trophy, is Ryan Dobson, who played for the Arizona Diamondbacks' minor-league affiliates in 2018 after a short time in the majors. The remaining boys are unidentified. (Courtesy of Víctor Alcalá.)

It's celebration time for the Westside Indians as they win the Víctory Athletic Baseball League championship in 2004 at Dodger Stadium. The league consisted of 32 teams with four divisions and was sponsored by Víctory Athletic, a uniform company in the San Fernando Valley. Players included Víctor Alcalá (lifting Eddie Morales) as well as Isaac Yoshinaga, Willie Holmes, Reed Algian, Brad Winklejohn, Lonnie Jackson, Jaime Carrillo, Dennis Hightower, Rubén Camacho, Ricardo Zamorano, Bobby Dobson, Mike McCaffrey, and Matt Levy. (Courtesy of Víctor Alcalá.)

At tournament play in 1977 in Palmdale, California, Frank Redondo throws the ball to first base. His team, the Graders, won the tournament. (Courtesy of Vince García Sr.)

Vince García Sr. comes in as a relief pitcher for the Graders during tournament play in Palmdale, California, in 1977. Rudy Romo was the starting ace pitcher, followed by Stan Busman. García was the bullpen relief pitcher, reliable in turning off the threatening fire. While a westside league team, the Graders participated in many travel tournaments throughout the year, playing in areas such as East Los Angeles, Arizona, and Las Vegas. (Courtesy of Vince García Sr.)

The tournament park director presents the championship trophy to Vince García Sr., manager, sponsor, and player with the Graders softball team in 1977. (Courtesy of Vince García Sr.)

Sammy Romo Jr., following in his father, Sammy Sr.'s, footsteps, played on many teams after his varsity play at Venice High School. A tagalong to his older brother Raymond, he was often asked to fill in and start at first base. He is known to have played on the Graders, the Oldies but Goodies, the Amazements, Patio Inn, and the Romo family baseball team. The family baseball legacy continued with his son Adam, who played varsity at Westchester High School and currently works at an instructional baseball school. (Courtesy of Vince García Sr.)

Rudy Romo (holding trophy) and nephew Raymond Romo celebrate another league championship in 1992. The team, sponsored by the Patio Inn, was undefeated in league play for five years. It was invited to leave the El Segundo League, as no other team could beat it. Other players on the team included Joey Carrillo, Mike González, John Huerta, Frank Redondo, Sammy Romo, and Greg Losman. Greg Losman's son J.P. Soto Losman played quarterback for the Buffalo Bills for three years. (Courtesy of Raymond Romo.)

Venice High alumni Raymond Romo (left) and Joey Carrillo played varsity baseball. They are pictured in the dugout at Centinela Park while playing in a B-league game. The Romos followed one another in playing for the same teams. Raymond played for the Graders, Patio Inn, the Oldies but Goodies, and the Amazements. Joey started out playing for the Truckers, followed by the Graders, the Indians, and the Amazements. Ballplayers who were exceptional, like the Romos and Joey Carrillo, played simultaneously on multiple competitive teams. (Courtesy of Raymond Romo.)

As a standout at St. Bernard's High School, Dan Melendez broke 14 school records in baseball. As a sophomore, he and his team went to the CIF championship game at Dodger Stadium. In 1989, at 17 years old, Melendez made the United States Junior National Team. This young US team won a gold medal in Canada. As a result of this series, Melendez was honored with the Most Valuable Player, Most Outstanding Player, and Most Outstanding First Baseman Awards. He accepted a full scholarship to Pepperdine. (Courtesy of Dan Melendez.)

As a junior in college, Dan Melendez and the 1992 Pepperdine Waves went to the College World Series in Omaha, Nebraska, where they beat the California State Fullerton Titans. Their coach was hall-of-famer Andy López. After this successful season, Melendez was drafted at No. 57 by the Los Angeles Dodgers. He played for the Bakersfield Dodgers, the San Antonio Missions (the Dodgers' AA team), and the Albuquerque Dukes (the Dodgers' AAA team). Jason Giambi was drafted by the Oakland A's after Melendez at No. 58. (Courtesy of Dan Melendez.)

This mostly unidentified 1958 Redlegs Major Division team played at Stoner Park in West Los Angeles in the Youth Baseball League. The player standing at center with the catcher's gear is Marcos Sánchez from West Los Angeles. A major corporate sponsor for youth baseball at Stoner Park, 7-Up provided hats and jerseys. Most of the players played baseball in dress or tennis shoes. The infield was never dragged, and there was never an umpire assigned to call the games, so a parent had to volunteer. (Courtesy of Jesse Sánchez.)

Richard Hernández was an All-City star at University High School in West Los Angeles. After high school, he was drafted in the minor leagues for Pittsburgh (one year) and then for the Baltimore Orioles in 1958. He signed his $25,000 contract in his parents' living room in the presence of his family, reporters, and his agent. A versatile player, he was able to play second and third base as well as shortstop. Baseball was in his blood, with his father Rufino playing on multiple teams in Santa Monica. As a young boy, Richard was the batboy of the 1946 Flowermen team in the Santa Monica chapter. The poem at the beginning of this book was written by Daniel Cano in tribute to his cousin Richard Hernández. (Courtesy of Daniel Cano.)

This 1965 men's team was sponsored by Alex's Men's Shop in West Los Angeles. From left to right are (first row) Danny Hernández, unidentified, and Joe Reynoso; (second row) unidentified, Brawley Estrada, ? Villa, Joe ?, and unidentified; (third row) Vince García Sr., Johnny ?, Rubén Estrada, Joey ?, and unidentified. Abie Carrillo was also known to have played with this team. Though a West Los Angeles team, it played at Memorial Park in Santa Monica for several seasons as a Division 3 team. (Courtesy of Vince García Sr.)

This Graders team was the 1974 champion of the West Los Angeles Stoner Park summer league and the Inglewood winter league. The team stayed together for at least eight years. Vince García Sr. was the sponsor. From left to right are (first row) Davey Valdez, Joey García, Vince García Sr., David Martínez, and Tommy Gómez; (second row) Chris Cruz, Ralph Romo, Vince García Jr., Larry Reyes, Pete Valdez Jr., Ron Vincent, and Mariano Molina. (Courtesy of Vince García Sr.)

Champions of the Los Angeles City League, Los Angeles City Tournament, City of Inglewood League, and their district, the Graders dominated softball in 1977. Part of their power and domination was the strength of their three pitchers. From left to right are (first row) Joey García, Raymond Romo, Vince García Sr., Vince García Jr., and Stan Busman; (second row) Rudy Romo, Greg Losman, Sammy Romo, Mariano Molina, Gilbert Sandoval, Chris Cruz, John Huerta, and John García. (Courtesy of Vince García Sr.)

Growing up in West Los Angeles, Jesse V. Sánchez played his first organized sports program at Stoner Recreation Center. He played sports at University High School, where he was awarded the first Mexican American Youth Organization Scholarship for baseball in 1964. After high school and serving in the military, he played in adult baseball and softball leagues. When Sánchez joined the District 25 Little League Board, he decided to enroll in umpiring courses. He was umpire in chief from 1989 to 2008 and umpired at all levels of baseball and softball in Culver City, West LA, Santa Monica, Del Rey, and Venice. Upon retirement, he became administrator of the District 25 Challengers Little League program and umpired all the games. (Courtesy of Jesse V. Sánchez.)

In 1969, Jesse V. Sánchez began coaching T-ball, and in 1974, he coached his first Major Division team. In 1984, he became the first Mexican American president of Culver American Little League until 1986. He held many positions in District 25 including assistant district administrator for both senior/big baseball and major/senior softball divisions. In June 1985, the board of the Culver American Little League named the field Jesse Sánchez Senior Field in his honor. (Courtesy of Jesse V. Sánchez.)

Bad Company, 1977 softball champions, won their tournament at Hazard Park in East Los Angeles. Pictured receiving the trophy are, from left to right (first row) Aurelio Carlos, unidentified Hazard Park director, Rubén Galván, and Tommy García; (second row) Ron Vincent, Johnny Van Boovan (barely visible), Louis Alcalá, and Larry Cruz; (third row) Pedro Garza, Tommy Gómez, and Frank Botello. Their home field was Stoner Park in West Los Angeles. Aurelio Carlos's business was the sponsor. This team played together for 10 years. (Courtesy of Ron Vincent.)

Santa Monica's Mina's Pizza restaurant sponsored this West Los Angeles team. This early 1980s Mina's team played slow-pitch softball. From left to right are (first row) Ernie Johnson, Tommy Gómez, Ernie Molina, unidentified, Mike González, Mariano Molina, and Davey Valdez; (second row) Pete Valdez Sr., Albert Piniedo, Bill Johnson, Paul Gómez, Bill Durn, Peter Valdez Jr., and Raúl González. Three sets of brothers played on this team—the Valdezes, Gómezes, and Molinas—as well as the Valdezes' father. (Courtesy of Tommy Gómez.)

UCLA is located in West Los Angeles. Angelica "Jelly" Félix was taken to a UCLA Bruins softball game as a child, and ever since, she dreamed of being a softball standout. She played four years of high school softball, and in 2013, while at UCLA, earned a spot on the PAC-12 Freshman Team as well as honorable mention as a walk-on. Pictured is her final collegiate at-bat, in which she singled in the Women's College World Series in Oklahoma City. (Courtesy of Angelica Félix.)

Playing third base, Angelica Félix was the last player to wear Jackie Robinson's No. 42 at UCLA before it was retired from all sports at the school. Like Robinson, Félix came from a modest background and was told she was too small and would not succeed in softball. Using Robinson as her motivation, she was determined to be the best softball player she could be, and succeeded in becoming a starter for the women's team. Since graduating, she has hosted softball clinics for underserved girls. (Courtesy of Angelica Félix.)

San Fernando Valley

Mexican American baseball has thrived in the Valley since the early 20th century. Remarkable players and teams received extensive coverage in Los Angeles newspapers. In the 1930s and 1940s, *La Opinion* credited San Fernando teams such as the Merchants, Blue Sox, and Martínez Café with helping to improve the economic, political, and social status of the Mexican American community. The San Fernando Missions emerged as one of the elite squads of the era. The Missions operated as a professional baseball club, featuring a board of directors that recruited top talent from across Southern California. Cofounded by Manuel Regalado and Juan Durazo, the organization included a business manager, Manuel Martínez, who paid players and arranged transportation for fans. The Canoga Park Merchants, under the guidance of managers Pete Rivera and Babe Valencia, gained recognition as a powerhouse in the region. Ray Barraza of Van Nuys drew so much attention setting strikeout records in the 1950s that the *Van Nuys Valley News* created a nickname for the softball pitcher, the "Buzz Bomb." Teams from Pacoima, North Hollywood, Sun Valley, Burbank, Glendale, Sunland-Tujunga, Northridge, and Chatsworth also garnered attention in the newspapers. Both male and female Mexican American high school athletes have graced the sports sections of the local papers, with many reaching the major leagues.

Baseball and softball propelled many players into leadership roles in the public sphere. In the late 1940s, articles credited Severiano "Babe" Valencia with instilling a strong sense of community in Canoga Park and called him the driving force behind baseball in the West Valley. Ritchie Encinas also held influential positions in West Valley municipal sports. Encinas became manager of the Reseda Merchants and served on several baseball and softball league boards of directors. The San Fernando Missions originally played on vacant lots within the San Fernando barrio, but under the leadership of managers Art Magaña and Pete Acebo, gained access to the major league quality San Fernando Park baseball diamond. Acebo was hired by the San Fernando Recreation Department in 1945. Through his years playing baseball as a member of the Pacoima Athletic Club, Pete Prieto managed to secure a position as assistant recreation director of Pacoima Park. Prieto was later hired as one of the first Mexican American Los Angeles police officers in 1949. Tony Servera transformed a vacant lot in the Orcasitas barrio of North Hollywood into a baseball diamond. He later helped build San Val Little League and has remained a well known figure in North Hollywood and Sun Valley.

The North Hollywood Vixies pose at the San Fernando American Legion on Mexican Independence Day in 1948. From left to right are (first row) Jennie Díaz, Dolores Moreno, Teresa Hernández, manager Ysabel "Chelo" Ramírez, Rámona Valenzuela, Lydia Sánchez, and Mary Hernández; (second row) Peggy Padilla, Lucy Castillo, Stella Quijada, Lupe Castillo, Rosie Chávez, Connie Lugo, and Julia Salazar. The Vixies played against the San Fernando Blue Jays, San Fernando Martínez Café, North Hollywood Huskies, and Pacoima Honeydrippers. Pitcher Rámona Valenzuela was team captain. (Courtesy of Mike Ramírez.)

These 1940s Burbank B Bops are, from left to right, (first row) Rámona Sarmiento, Rosie Díaz, Jean Snyder, Margaret Moreno, and Margaret Escudero; (second row) Tencha Moreno, Eleanor Roblero, Eleanor Yáñez, Judy Davila, Lupe Díaz, and unidentified. Baseball and softball provided opportunities for Mexican American women to interact. Women met lifelong friends whether as teammates or opposing players. Rosie Díaz lived on the outskirts of town and met her teammates while attending Burbank High School. In Burbank, Mexican Americans could not buy property north of Glenoaks Boulevard. Despite their exclusion from certain movie theaters and swimming pools, Burbank Mexican American teams played at city parks. The B Bops played at Olive Recreation Center in Burbank. The St. Louis Browns trained at the same park. (Courtesy of Rosie Díaz and Alex Sáenz.)

Tony Servera stands at left next to Willie Mays during opening day at San Val Little League in May 1965. In 1940, Servera constructed a ballfield on a vacant lot in the Orcasitas barrio of North Hollywood. In 1958, he helped build San Val Little League in Sun Valley, transforming a former city dump into a thriving youth league. He founded a concrete company in 1957 that is currently in its third generation of family ownership. The multi-million-dollar company worked on the Beverly Hills City Hall, Natural History Museum of Los Angeles, and Will Rogers State Beach. (Courtesy of Los Angeles Public Library Photo Collection.)

The North Hollywood Wolves feast after a game in the late 1950s. From left to right are Frank Castillo, Tommy Chávez, Bill Chávez, Inéz Reyes, George Alvarado, Chris Sánchez, Ray González, manager Percy Ramírez, Wesley ?, ? Reyes, Aurelio Enciso, John Lara, Joey Díaz, unidentified, Víctor Ramírez, Tony Velarde, and Anthony Servera. (Courtesy of Mike Velarde.)

Gathered in 1937 at Calisto Muro's house are, from left to right, Blas Muro, Clementina Placito, Mary Muro, Antonia Almeida, Consuelo Ávila, Helen Cortéz, Lola Ávila, Amparo Muro, and Enadina Álvarez. The North Hollywood barrio was east of Vineland Avenue, south of Burbank Boulevard, and north of Magnolia Boulevard. Families later moved to the nearby Orcasitas barrio and new suburban tracts in Sun Valley. The area now consists of industrial structures. Santa Susanna Mission still stands and operates as an antiques store. (Courtesy of Abel Pérez.)

Pictured in 1940, San Fernando Missions player Abelino "Joe" Pérez stands near his house on Satsuma Avenue in North Hollywood. Born in Madera, California, in 1919, Pérez settled in North Hollywood in the 1930s. The family previously lived in the California Central Valley, Arizona, and Sinaloa, México. Pérez served in the Army at Camp Roberts during World War II. He married Adela Ponce from a longstanding San Fernando Valley family. Her cousins managed the Lankershim Ranch in North Hollywood from the 1920s to the 1950s. (Courtesy of Abel Pérez.)

This 1940s Lankershim Village Club (LVC) included, from left to right, (first row) batboys Rudy Madrid, Víctor Ramírez, and Alfred "Beaver" Moreno; (second row) Ysabel "Chelo" Ramírez, David Alderete, Tommy Díaz, William Moreno, Mike Alderete, and Manuel Díaz; (third row) Mark Montoya, Bill Chávez, Frank Salas, Al Márquez, Tony Servera, Dan Padilla, Vince Sánchez, and manager Percy Ramírez. In 1950, the team unsuccessfully petitioned the Los Angeles City Council for a playground. (Courtesy of Mike Velarde.)

Teammates and friends Ernie Gonzáles (left) and Mike Alderete pose in the 1950s. Alderete lived in the Orcasitas barrio. He received attention from professional baseball scouts while playing on teams such as LVC, US Steel, and Sun Valley Monarchs. His brother David played on these teams and for the North Hollywood Cubs youth team. Mike Alderete served three years as a corporal in the Army during World War II. Ernie Gonzáles served in World War II as a staff sergeant in the infantry in Luzon, Philippines, and stayed on duty in Japan after the dropping of the atomic bombs. He received several awards, including the Silver Star. (Courtesy of Speedy Gonzáles.)

Members of the 1940s Van Nuys High School Girls Athletic Association (GAA) team are, from left to right, Lydia Pacheco, Delia Durazo, Hope Santellano, and Inéz Gutíerrez. Hope Santellano graduated from Van Nuys High School in 1949 as GAA club captain, receiving a letter and two stripes. Lydia Pacheco met husband Vince Sánchez, from North Hollywood, while playing in a softball game. (Courtesy of Hope Santellano Alcalá.)

Hope Santellano is pictured as a young girl in the 1930s. She is standing outside her home along with her mother, Maria Galván Santellano (left), and aunt Heleria Santellano Fabela. As a child, Hope helped can the produce and dried corn to make *chuales*. She attended the segregated Lemona Avenue School for Mexicans in Van Nuys. Lemona Avenue was demolished and rebuilt as Sylvan Park Elementary School. Mexican Americans in Van Nuys were barred from swimming pools except for the occasional International Day, when the city opened the pools to nonwhites. (Courtesy of Hope Santellano Alcalá.)

California Brick & Tile of Van Nuys sponsored this 1930s women's team. They are, from left to right, (first row) Lupe Vásquez (sitting in truck), Grace Cano (standing in front), unidentified, Josie Pacheco, and Sophia Vásquez (sitting on hood); (second row, standing on truck bed) Phyllis Martínez, unidentified, Eleanor Martínez, and Else Pacheco (sitting on top). Phyllis and Eleanor Martínez's younger sister, Irene, played for the Van Nuys Duchesses softball team. (Courtesy of Irene García.)

Virginia Ruiz Durazo (left) and sister-in-law Connie Ruiz pose in this World War II–era photograph. They are wearing the Van Nuys Merchants jerseys belonging to their husbands, who were serving overseas. The Ruiz family settled in Los Angeles in the 1800s and were listed in the 1870 US Census. They originally lived in the Chinatown section of Los Angeles between College, Alpine, and Yale Streets. Durazo's father was born at the San Gabriel Mission and later moved to Simons (now Montebello), where Virginia was born. The family moved to Van Nuys in the early 1920s, living in one of the first houses built in the growing suburb. At one time, the Ruiz family owned extensive land in Los Angeles County and present-day Thousand Oaks. (Courtesy of Virginia Ruiz Durazo.)

The 1930s Van Nuys Merchants team included Julian Barraza, Johnny Cano, Ralph Durazo, Louie Gonzáles, Ángel Guajardo, Joe Hurtado, batboy Danny Pacheco, Mike Pacheco, Rupert Pacheco, Mike Palacios, Frank Ruiz, Tommy Ruiz, Tacho Santellano, and Joe Ybarra. Rupert Pacheco graduated in 1935 from Van Nuys High School, where he won numerous football awards. One of his football trophies is displayed at Van Nuys High School. Pacheco won a medal in a track race at the Los Angeles Coliseum. (Courtesy of Virginia Ruiz Durazo.)

Van Nuys Merchants players and friends Joe Ybarra (left) and Mike Palacios pose in 1942. Palacios was born in 1915 in Kingsburg, Fresno County, where his parents were seasonal agricultural workers. Ybarra worked at the California Brick & Tile factory. Teams played on a field next to the brickyard, which was located at 6151 Kester Avenue in the Van Nuys barrio. Originally named Owens Brick Co., the factory opened in the 1920s and provided work for many families. By the 1960s, the plant produced 40,000–130,000 bricks per day. The company moved its plant to Castaic in 1969. Auto garages and industrial buildings now occupy the former site of the brickyard. Van Nuys men's teams in the 1930s and 1940s included the Merchants, Black Demons, Alyce Blue Gown, and California Brick Company. Players included Cardoza, Cortinas, Cruz, Enríquez, Fonseca, Moreno, and Robles. (Courtesy of Mike Palacios Jr.)

Joe Ponce Jr. stands in his Smith's Café uniform in 1953. The team competed in the Valley Municipal League. The Van Nuys native received a contract offer from the Angels of the Pacific Coast League. He experienced prejudice at Van Nuys High School and only played for the junior varsity team. Ponce was stationed at Fort Ord during the Korean War. His father, Joe Ponce Sr., trained the famous Pacoima boxer Bobby Chacón. (Courtesy of Virginia Ruiz Durazo and Reggie Ponce.)

Pitcher Ray Barraza (left) and catcher Andy Durazo are seen in the 1960s as members of the Tom Carrell Chevrolet softball team. Andy's father, Juan Durazo, was the inaugural manager and president of the San Fernando Missions. Prior to moving to San Fernando in the 1920s, Juan Durazo lived in Tombstone, Arizona, and worked in the silver mines. Andy Durazo, an employee at Tom Carrell Chevrolet, organized the team. Durazo was a noted softball catcher and power hitter in the 1960s and also played for a Mattson's sponsored team in San Fernando. He sold cars for many years and later owned disposal companies. Ray Barraza, nicknamed the "Buzz Bomb," received frequent coverage in the *Van Nuys Valley News*. In 1954, he struck out a record 212 batters in the Major Softball Association, winning the Most Valuable Player and Strikeout King awards, and was scouted by the Chicago White Sox. (Courtesy of Joffee García Jr.)

This late 1940s Pacoima Athletic Club consisted of, from left to right, (first row) George Villanueva, Sylvester Cancino, Pete Prieto, batboy Alfred J. Calzada, Raymond Pacheco, Poncho Torres, and Eddie Prieto; (second row) Nacho Calzada, Símon Salas, Ángel Luna, unidentified, Del Rey, Ted Villanueva, and James "Jimmy" García. García was born in 1917 in Lompoc, California, and played baseball at Lompoc High School. He played on Lompoc and Santa Maria community teams before moving to Pacoima in 1944. (Courtesy of Pete Prieto.)

This 1940s Pacoima Athletic Club team photograph shows, from left to right, (first row) Símon Salas, Sylvester Cancino, George Villanueva, batboy Alfred J. Calzada, Félix Villegas, Pete Almeida, unidentified batboy, and unidentified; (second row) Nacho Calzada, Ángel Luna, Pete Prieto, Eddie Prieto, Raymond Pacheco, and unidentified; (third row) Ted Villanueva, Poncho Torres, and Del Rey. The power-hitting duo of brothers Eddie and Pete Prieto drew interest from major-league scouts. Eddie once hit a home run off future Dodger pitcher Don Drysdale. (Courtesy of Josephine Cancino and Irene Rodríguez.)

In the summer of 1942, eighteen-year-old Pacoima native Pete Prieto enlisted in the Marine Corps. Soon after he embarked for the Pacific theater, traveling 6,700 miles on a supply ship to a Marine base in New Zealand. Serving with the 2nd Marine Division in the motor transport division, Prieto was present at the Battle of Tarawa in November 1943. After Tarawa, he was stationed with brother Eddie at Saipan in the Mariana Islands. The brothers remained together off the Okinawa coast until kamikazes hit Eddie's ship at the Battle of Okinawa in 1945. Eddie survived the attack and took refuge in China before returning safely to the United States. Pete Prieto retired as a corporal in January 1946 and settled back into civilian life in Pacoima with his wife, Carmen. (Courtesy of Pete and Marsha Prieto.)

Pictured in the 1940s, Ángel Hernández (center) holds his father's baseball glove. His father, Lupe G. Hernández (right), was born in Amarillo, Texas, moving to Pacoima as a child in 1919. Ángel played for years at Las Palmas Park in San Fernando. After graduating from San Fernando High School in 1964, he served in the Vietnam War with the 101st Airborne Division. His brother John Hernández played on the Paxton Park All-Stars that won the East Valley in the early 1960s. In the championship game against Panorama City, John hit a crucial home run to help win the game. Lupe's daughter, Terry, became a star player for softball teams including Sylmar Las Muñecas. (Courtesy of Terry Hernández.)

This 1930s Pacoima softball team featured, from left to right, (first row) Julián Almeida, Joe Escalante, Louie García, and Jimmy Hernández; (second row) unidentified, Lupe G. Hernández, Pete Almeida, unidentified, Nacho Calzada, and Joe Martínez; (third row) Joe Moreno, Albert Escalante, Jack Moreno, unidentified, and Eddie Prieto. After serving with the Merchant Marines during World War II, Louie García organized community events mentoring at-risk youth through the Catholic Youth Organization and Teen Post. (Courtesy of Joffee García Jr.)

The 1936 Pacoima Aztecas featured Della Fonseca (second row, second from right). Fonseca was descended from the Rosas family, one of the first 11 *pobladores* families that founded El Pueblo de la Reina de Los Angeles in 1781. Like most women who played softball, she made lifelong friends among teammates and opposing players. With an average attendance of 3,000 per game, 340,000 people paid to see womens' softball in 1938 in Los Angeles. (Courtesy of Los Angeles Public Library Photo Collection.)

This 1930s Studio City team included Mexican American players from throughout the Valley: Tony Murillo from Canoga Park (first row kneeling, far left), Nacho Calzada from Pacoima (second row standing, second from left), and Severiano "Babe" Valencia from Canoga Park (second row, second from right). In many areas of the Valley prior to World War II, Mexican Americans could not play baseball at municipal parks unless they played for white teams. Canoga Park Mexican American teams constructed a diamond on the corner of Deering Avenue and Gault Street. (Courtesy of Arnold Murillo.)

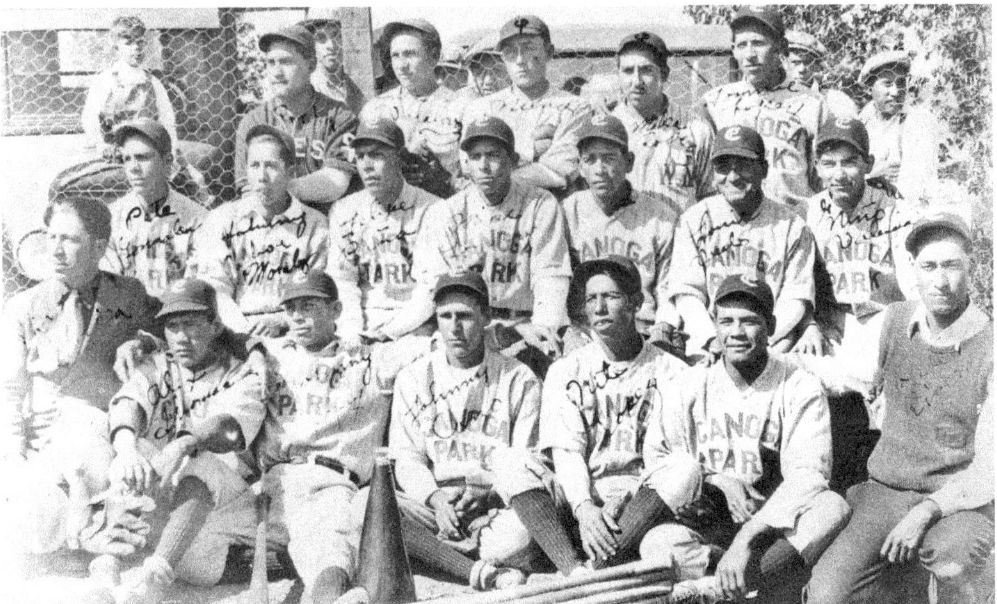

These 1930s Canoga Park Merchants are, from left to right, (first row) two unidentified, Johnny López, Johnny Cano, Nito López, Joe Miranda, and manager Pete Rivera; (second row) Pete Gonzáles, Johnny Morales, Felipe Piña, Mike Gonzáles, two unidentified, and Severiano "Babe" Valencia; (third row) ? Rocha, Louis Villalovoz, two unidentified, and Tommie López. (Courtesy of William Rivera.)

This late 1940s Canoga Park Merchants team is, from left to right, (first row) unidentified, Joe Miranda, Severiano "Babe" Valencia, ? Sutton, and Mike Gonzáles; (second row) Tony Murillo, three unidentified, Tex Simpson, Vic Gonzáles, and Joe Argott. Skilled catcher and first baseman Tony Murillo was born in Tempe, Arizona, in 1919 and moved to Canoga Park in the 1930s. Tony and brother Joe Murillo played on Sunday teams throughout the 1930s–1950s. Other Canoga Park players from this era included the Acostas, Alphonso Argott, B. Argott, Lefty Cordova, Ritchie Encinas, Alex Franco, Raúl Franco, Joe Gonzáles, Tony Gonzáles, Jover, Levario, R. Miranda, Morelete, Parente, Serrano, and Jim Smith. (Courtesy of Sylvia Valencia Wiltz.)

These 1930s Canoga Park Babe Valencia All Stars included, from left to right, (first row) Pedro Gonzáles, David Vaiz, Mike Gonzáles, manager Severiano "Babe" Valencia, Joe Yescas, Óscar Franco, and John Bracamonte; (second row) unidentified, Tom Eastburn, Tex Simpson, Paul Franco, three unidentified, and Raymond Rivera. Raymond Rivera's father, Pete, was the original manager of the Canoga Park Merchants. Early teams in Canoga Park included the Cubs, Indians, and Canoga Citrus. (Courtesy of Sylvia Valencia Wiltz.)

Canoga Park Merchants manager Severiano "Babe" Valencia (left) poses with Merchants player and compadre Raymond "Monchi" Rivera in the late 1940s. Raymond Rivera played on the Canoga Park Merchants from 1947 to 1953. An accomplished athlete at Canoga Park High School, Rivera earned three letters in both baseball and basketball. He wrote for the school newspaper, the *Hunters Call*, becoming the sports editor during his senior year in 1948–1949. He coached the Red Devils, a Catholic Youth Organization basketball team that played at the Guadalupe Community Center. (Courtesy of Raymond Rivera and Marie Armenta.)

These softball players at the Canoga Park Our Lady of Guadalupe Youth Center in the 1950s are, from left to right, Jennie Trujillo, Sister Bernadette, Mary Lou Reyes, Eloise Cruz (kneeling), Mary Lou Pérez, Ofilia Beltrán, and Dolly Pérez. In the background are, from left to right, Joe Carlin (riding bicycle), Danny Cordova, Jess Hernández, and Herman Murillo. Mary Orcutt, a wealthy landowner in Canoga Park, deeded land to the Archdiocese of Los Angeles to provide recreational activities "for youths of Mexican ancestry." Dedicated in 1950, the Canoga Park Our Lady of Guadalupe Youth Center remains a vital institution in the community. (Courtesy of Amador Espinoza.)

The 1949 Chatsworth boys softball championship team included Alphonso "Gillette" Argott Jr. (second row, third from left, wearing his father's Army jacket). A descendant of an old-time San Fernando Valley family, Argott grew up in Chatsworth. He played catcher at Canoga Park High School. His father, Alphonso Sr., played on early Canoga Park baseball teams and umpired in the Valley. Alphonso Jr. served in the US Navy from 1951 to 1954. (Courtesy of Jo Argott and Naomi Talamantes.)

San Fernando Valley communities also formed football teams. Many of the players on this early 1960s Canoga Park team, sponsored by Clem Ruh Chevrolet, played park, Little League, and high school baseball. From left to right are, (first row, kneeling) Jess Trejo, Armando Cota, Robert Campos, and Danny Argott; (second row, standing) Edward "Beaver" Alamillo, Richard Perea, Alex Hernández, Joe Trejo, Mike Leon, Frank Vargas, Pete Ramírez, and unidentified. Art Sánchez coached the team and worked for the CYO Guadalupe Center as a sports instructor. The extensive Argott family has produced numerous Canoga Park athletes for decades. Danny Argott's grandchildren Lilliana, Lisette, Angeline, Andrew, Robert, Marissa, and Vinny Argott received athletic honors at Canoga Park High School. (Courtesy of Amador Espinoza.)

The Canoga Park Louie's Market team started around 1967–1968. In 1972, it consisted of, from left to right, (first row) John Espinoza, Tony Díaz, Alfred Murillo, Jess Trejo, and Frank Sotelo; (second row) Ray García, Arnold Murillo, Eddie Rubio, Bobby Ochoa, and Frankie Árias; (third row) Roy Slay, Ron St. Marie, Plus Amper, and Jesse Hernández. (Courtesy of Laura and Robert Ochoa.)

Canoga Park High School ace pitcher Richard Gallegos winds up in 1962. Gallegos started playing baseball at Canoga Park Little League in 1955. With great support from his family, he continued playing baseball every year until high school. At Canoga Park High School, he received three varsity letters and was chosen Co-Senior of the Year along with teammate Augie Cirrito. His brother Robert Gallegos also played for Canoga Park High School. Richard passed his love of baseball to his sons—Joel, Richard Jr., and Joe—who all participated in youth baseball leagues. A standout player, Joe Gallegos won the Golden Glove as second baseman for the Simi Valley High School Pioneers team that won the 1987 league championship. That year, the team was invited to Florida for the Colonial Tournament, where it finished in second place. (Courtesy of Richard Gallegos.)

First baseman Arnold Murillo won West Valley Player of the Year and All-City honors at Canoga Park High School in 1967. He was drafted by the Atlanta Braves but did not sign. He played two years at Los Angeles Valley College, earning All-Conference awards in 1968 and 1969, then made the Big Sky All-Conference team at Gonzaga and led the Bulldogs in hitting. He played competitive softball in Burbank for the Congress League. In 1977, his team won the International Softball Congress world championship. Brothers Herman, Alfred, and Billy all excelled at baseball and football at Canoga Park High. Father Tony Murillo was a well-known Canoga Park ballplayer in the 1930s and 1940s. (Courtesy of Arnold Murillo.)

Ritchie Encinas moved to the small agricultural town of Reseda in the 1930s, one of the few Mexican Americans in the area. He quickly made an impression as the lone Mexican American on the Reseda Merchants, leading the team to the 1939 Los Angeles Municipal League championship. He served as a leading Reseda representative on numerous baseball and softball league boards of directors and was manager in the prestigious *Van Nuys News* West Valley All-Star game played in front of 3,500 at Reseda Park in 1949. Encinas also played for Northridge and Canoga Park teams. El Barrio de Los Compadres was located at the current site of Cal State University at Northridge. (Courtesy of Richard F. Encinas and Armida Encinas.)

This 1930 Chatsworth team, likely named the Merchants or Athletics, stands in front of Stoney Point. It includes Jose Jiménez (far left), Mac Ramírez (second from left), and José Castañeda (fourth from left). Several *La Opinión* articles covered the team, comprising players from Chatsworth and Canoga Park. Box scores list Altamirano, Balta, Bustamante, Esparza, González, Ortiz, Parente, N. Ramírez, T. Ramírez, Téllez, Valencia, and Vargas as players. The team played the Tucson Tigers (Vernon), Cuauhtémoc (Los Angeles), Roger Jessup Farm (Glendale), Pico Court Blues (San Fernando), Pacoima, and Agoura Americans. (Courtesy of Rachel Jiménez and Art Castañeda.)

The Sunkist (lemon) packinghouse–Blue Goose (orange) packinghouse championship game was held at San Fernando Park in 1932. The Blue Goose team, from the Hazeltine Packing House on Truman Street, won the title. The game drew an immense crowd from the San Fernando community. Players include Refugio Samora (first row, fourth from left), Manuel A. Castro (first row, sixth from left, sitting on bench) and Arthur Lyon (first row, third from right). According to a 1944 *Los Angeles Times* article, the San Fernando Valley contained over 11,000 acres of lemon, orange, and grapefruit orchards along with 10 packinghouses. (Courtesy of Marianne Castro Lawson.)

The newly formed San Fernando Missions are pictured at White Sox Park in 1932. From left to right are (first row) Juan Durazo (team president), Lefty Ocampo, John García, Alonzo "Pops" Orozco, two unidentified, and David Cruz; (second row) unidentified, Refugio Samora, two unidentified, manager Manuel Regalado, unidentified, Pinney García, and two unidentified. According to box scores, other players on this team included ? Calderón, Cecil Cruz, Tommy Enríquez, Chico Manríquez, ? Moreno, ? Rivera, Gene Rodríguez, and Pete Salazar. The Missions consisted of players hailing from all over Los Angeles. (Courtesy of Joffee García Jr.)

These late 1930s San Fernando Monarchs at White Sox Park are, from left to right, (first row) Joe Ponce, unidentified, Félix Bustamante, unidentified, Robert Uribe, and Elijio Salas; (second row) Adolpho Rocha, unidentified, Joe Miranda, Ernie "Lefty" Ríos, manager Art Magaña, Frank Pérez, actor Chris-Pin Martín, Jess Franco, Marin Magaña, John García, and Pinney García. The park, at Thirty-Eighth Street and Compton Avenue in South Los Angeles, hosted tournaments featuring top Mexican American and visiting Mexican clubs. These matchups were important diplomatic displays as part of the Good Neighbor Policy of the 1930s. Attendees included movie stars of the day such as Lupita Tovar and Chris-Pin Martín. (Courtesy of Pinney García Jr.)

Pictured in 1940 on Satuma Avenue in North Hollywood are, from left to right, Abelino "Joe" Pérez, unidentified, Willie Pérez, Lupita Pérez, and unidentified. Willie Pérez received a Purple Heart during World War II. Lupita worked dispatch for the Los Angeles Police Department Foothill Division. The San Fernando Missions included a board of directors comprising Juan Durazo (president), Manuel Martínez (business manager), Pablo Ramírez (secretary), Francisco López (treasurer), Amado "Chief" Herrera (manager), and Art Magaña (manager). In 1932, Martínez paid for a fleet of trucks to transport hundreds of San Fernando fans to watch the Missions play at White Sox Park. The team fielded major-league talent such as George Vico and Melo Almada. (Courtesy of Abel Pérez.)

Crispin "Pinney" García is pictured at San Fernando Park in the late 1940s. As a young child in the 1910s, García and his family moved to San Fernando from Guanajuato, México. He was a mainstay in center field for the Missions and other San Fernando teams along with his brothers John, Joe, and David. Pinney also played for the San Fernando Blue Sox, San Fernando Monarchs, Sunland-Tujunga Merchants, and Pico Court Blues. Situated on the outskirts of San Fernando, Pico Court housed citrus workers in adobe houses and included a general store, dancehall, and bar. Pico Court was demolished in the 1960s for the construction of the 118 freeway. García later competed in the Mexican League and tried out for the Los Angeles Angels of the Pacific Coast League. (Courtesy of Alicia Serra Stevens and Ray Serra Jr.)

The 1947 San Fernando Missions pose for a team picture in the bleachers at San Fernando Park. From left to right are (first row) Ralph Hernández, Leo Guerra, Ángel Guajardo, manager Art Magaña, Joe Thomas, and Frank Parra; (second row) Félix Guajardo, Joe García, Nick Salas, Ernie Ortiz, and Mario Vásquez. Many players commuted from Santa Monica, such as Ángel and Félix Guajardo, Ralph Hernández, and Mario Vásquez. Art Magaña took over the Missions in the 1940s. Born in 1914 in Guanajuato, México, Magaña moved to San Fernando as a child, living on Kalisher Street. (Courtesy of Alicia Serra Stevens and Ray Serra Jr.)

The San Fernando Missions play at San Fernando Park in 1947. Joffee García is at left wearing his catching equipment. The San Fernando Missions and Monarchs originally played on vacant lots at street intersections. Built in 1936 as a Work Progress Administration project, San Fernando Park became the spring training home of the Seattle Rainiers and Hollywood Stars. Games featured mariachi music. (Courtesy of David Magaña.)

This 1951 San Fernando High School Tigers varsity team includes B. Barragán (first row, second from left), Raúl Espinoza (first row, third from left), J. Negrete (second row, second from left), and David García (second row, fourth from left). Catcher Espinoza lettered in baseball and football for the Tigers. Son Robert Espinoza starred at Sylmar High and made the 1974 All–East Valley First Team. David García played for the Hollywood Stars. In 2009, his grandson David García III was drafted by the Dodgers out of Kennedy High School in Granada Hills. (Courtesy of San Fernando Valley Historical Society.)

Robert "Bob" Bórquez grew up in a longtime San Fernando baseball family. Father Anastacio and uncle Alphonso played on early teams. Bob enlisted in the Army after graduating from San Fernando High in 1945. Nicknamed "Mighty Mouse" for his power hitting, he played on US Army softball teams while stationed in Cologne, Germany. His son Danny played military baseball while stationed in South Korea in 1967. Danny has coached his children and grandchildren for years at Sylmar Independent Baseball League and North Valley Pony League. His travel teams, the Mid-Valley SoCal Bears and Simi Stars, won back-to-back Cooperstown Dreams Park tournament championships, beating out 104 teams. (Courtesy of Robert Bórquez.)

John Fonseca is pictured in his 508th Airborne Regiment softball uniform in 1952. Fonseca received multiple letters as a pitcher at San Fernando High and once pitched a no-hitter against Verdugo Hills High School. His regiment, nicknamed the "Red Devils," was stationed at Fort Benning, Georgia, from 1951 to 1953 during the Korean War. He played against military teams from Fort Jackson, South Carolina, and Miami, Florida. In 1954, Fonseca was transferred to Fort Campbell, Kentucky. He played for the San Fernando Merchants alongside Eddie Sierra, Bob Hernández, Bruce Erickson, Ritchie Ortiz, and Jess Franco. Fonseca has worked as a barber since the late 1950s. (Courtesy of John Fonseca.)

After graduating from Canoga Park High School in 1963, Richard Gallegos joined the US Marine Corps and was stationed at Camp Pendleton with the 2nd Battalion, 5th Marines. His Marine baseball team won the division. He deployed to Danang, South Vietnam, in 1965, serving with the 2nd Battalion, 3rd Marines, until 1966. He played and coached baseball with his brother Robert. (Courtesy of Richard Gallegos.)

In 1958, Bobby Luján won All-Valley and All-City First Team awards as third baseman at San Fernando High School. Luján hit one of the longest home runs in Valley League history, well over 400 feet at San Fernando Park. Luján played on a Dodgers prospect team organized by scout Mike Brito. He played softball in the General Motors League, leading the UAW 645 Boppers to a championship. Uncle Esequiel "Chapo" Aguilar played on the 1930s Pacoima Merchants. (Courtesy of San Fernando Valley Historical Society.)

The 1962 Tom Carrell Chevrolet championship team includes, from left to right, (first row) Richard Hidalgo and Tony Márquez; (second row) unidentified, Rubén L. Ruiz, Jack Mayer, Brian ?, Ray Barraza, Fidel Guerrero, Jess Barraza, Andy Durazo, and Tony Flores. Other players include Ernie Castro, Raúl Espinoza, Mike Hidalgo, Mickey Valdez, Mike Durazo, Jim Durazo, Bob Chávez, and Chuck Tisher. They won the title against the G.C. Breidert team. Ray Barraza, widely regarded as the greatest softball pitcher in San Fernando Valley history, gave up one hit for the victory. (Courtesy of Mike and Efrenia Hidalgo.)

A 1960s General Motors UAW team poses at San Fernando Park. From left to right are (first row) Bob Martínez, Manuel Vaiz, unidentified, R. Orduno, Tommy Fasanella, and Dave ?; (second row) Harold "Quack" Vaiz, David Vaiz, Ray Guerrero, Henry Real, unidentified, Tony Torres, and unidentified. Home run hitter Manuel Vaiz worked at Van Nuys General Motors in the paint department for 35 years. Pete Beltrán, a former baseball standout at San Fernando High, became the first Chicano UAW 645 president in 1978 and led a successful campaign to keep Van Nuys General Motors open another 10 years. (Courtesy of Irene Vaiz.)

The Orioles won the local UAW softball title in 1974. From left to right are (first row) Danny García, Bobby Estrada, manager John Álcantar, Clarence Blakely, and Jack Ballard; (second row) Bob Calzada, Danny Alvarado, Augie Martínez, Jess Álvarez, Jim Dixon, Earl Cook, and Tommy Tapia Jr. Manager and pitcher John Álcantar guided the team to an undefeated record. Estrada worked in most departments at the plant. His father, Natividad, played on the 1940 San Fernando High School team, while his son Bobby Jr. played in the Sylmar Independent Baseball League and Mission Hills Little League. (Courtesy of Terry Hernández and Joffee García Jr.)

Chris Vaiz is seen pitching for College of the Canyons in Santa Clarita. Vaiz starred at Alemany High School in Mission Hills, graduating in 1978. He also wrestled and played football in high school. Vaiz was offered a baseball scholarship to the University of San Francisco and was scouted by the Giants and Cubs. He later played for Anahuac in the Mexican League. The longstanding Vaiz family of San Fernando has fielded countless baseball and softball athletes, including Chris's father, Manuel Vaiz. Among many others are Alex, David, Harold, Isabelle, Jennie, Josephine, Luis, Mike, Paul, and Pete Vaiz. (Courtesy of Irene Vaiz.)

Armando Madrid started as a coach in the Sylmar Independent Baseball League and at Las Palmas Park in San Fernando in the 1960s–1970s. He helped guide the California State University, Northridge (CSUN), women's softball team to a 1984 NCAA Division II championship. Daughter Christina Madrid played for CSUN, while daughter Pauline went to Sacred Heart College in Connecticut. His other daughter, Annette, played in various softball leagues. All three played softball at Kennedy High School in Granada Hills, where they won a city title. Madrid tutored well-known softball players such as Jessica Mendoza and Lori Harrigan. (Courtesy of Adela Almeida Madrid.)

Ignacio "Nacho" Díaz served in the Army during World War II and the Korean War. He saw heavy combat during both wars, suffering a wound to his leg. He received Purple Heart and marksmanship awards. Nacho played on the Pacoima Potter Milling company team and other teams in the 1930s and 1940s. He kept his old baseball jerseys in his truck. Sons Richard, Clem, and Roy played at Pacoima Little League, San Fernando Babe Ruth League, San Fernando High School, and softball leagues at Las Palmas Park. (Courtesy of Richard Díaz.)

THE GOLDEN STATE

This is the 11th book documenting the vast and splendid memories of Mexican American baseball and softball in the Golden State. Previous books have centered on Los Angeles, the Inland Empire, Orange County, the Central Coast, the Pomona Valley, the San Fernando Valley, Ventura County, East Los Angeles, the San Gabriel Valley, Sacramento, and now the Westside of Los Angeles. Nearly 4,000 photographs have been highlighted thus far. California Mexican Americans, since at least 1870, have had a birthright to baseball and softball at all levels of play including youth, high school, college, community, workplace, military, women, semi-professional and professional, church, and in México.

Yet these impressive pictures and remarkable stories represent a mere glimpse of the full history of baseball in the state with the most Mexican Americans. Several areas and regions have not yet been sufficiently investigated, including the South Bay, the San Francisco–Oakland area, Imperial County, the Víctorville-Barstow region, San Diego, the Santa Maria region, South Central Los Angeles, the Central Valley, and the far north region. Nevertheless, images from these areas have been integrated in previous books, including specific chapters on San Diego, the Central Valley, and the Santa Maria Valley, but much more research is required.

Another area that is often overlooked is between the Inland Empire and the Pomona Valley. This region includes the communities of Bloomington, Fontana, Rialto, Upland, and Ontario. A small number of Upland and Ontario photographs have been incorporated in earlier books. There are several Bloomington images in this chapter, and aggressive steps are being taken to find more from these important neighborhoods for upcoming books.

There are still many exceptional photographs and stories that need exploring, documenting, publishing, and promoting. Mexican Americans have had a vibrant impact on social, political, economic, cultural, and recreational life in California. As these books have clearly shown, baseball and softball for Mexican Americans and other Spanish-speaking groups have been equally essential as casting a ballot, forming a labor union, establishing a business, promoting gay rights, supporting gender equality, graduating from school, defending the nation, serving on a jury, endorsing immigrant rights, and running for public office. Indeed, the ballfield has been a community forum where all these sectors converge on Sunday, planning and enhancing their effective strategies for equal opportunity and social justice.

The city of Bloomington is located in San Bernardino County, neighboring Fontana, Rialto, and Upland. The 1997 Houston Astros, led by head coach Ray Solis Sr. (second row, far left) and his son Ray Jr. (second row, far right) are pictured with Jeremy Solis, (second row, third from left). Players from left to right are Jarred ?, Brian Peña, Jeremy Solis, John ?, Ricardo ?, Erick Carrillo, and Albert Gómez. (Courtesy of Jessica Carrillo.)

The 2000 Bloomington Junior Division Tigers were a well-coached team. Coaches, team moms, and snack bar workers consisted mostly of volunteers from the community. Many teams consisted of extended family members. Players pictured here are, from left to right, (first row) two unidentified, Jeremy Solis, Ernie Gómez, and Jessica Carrillo; (second row) Erick Carrillo, Dante ?, unidentified, and Michael ? The three coaches are unidentified. Longtime friendships were created over the years. (Courtesy of Jessica Carrillo.)

The unselfish dedication displayed by baseball parents is a reflection of their values, along with the commitment that crosses generations in Bloomington families. Seen here in 2000 are team mom Chris Reed (second row, second from left), coach Michael Alexander (second row, far left), his son Mikey Alexander (second row, third from left), coach Mario Silva (second row, far right), and his son Rubén Silva (second row, second from right). (Courtesy of Jessica Carrillo.)

This 2001 team included many players from various teams in Bloomington Little League. The boys are all between 14 and 16 years old. All-star games often drew the biggest crowds and required specific lighting to be in place for night games. The crowds could be heard several blocks away. The brightly colored All-Star uniforms distinguished the players during these high-stakes games. (Courtesy of Jessica Carrillo.)

Childhood friendships from Bloomington have continued well into teenage years and beyond. Pictured here are best friends and neighbors (from left to right) Rubén Silva, Erick Carrillo, his sister Jessica Carrillo, and Richard Soria. Jessica Carrillo was one of a few girls playing in Bloomington Little League at this time. The rare sight of a girl playing baseball in the league was unthinkable. The boys continued playing for many years at Kessler Park. Less than a handful of girls played baseball during the 1990s. (Courtesy of Jessica Carrillo.)

Today, the Little League program is the longest running youth sports program (baseball and softball) in Bloomington. Erick Carrillo began playing at seven years old in the farm division and later played in high school and at the University of Riverside, Riverside City College, and California State University, San Bernardino. He played shortstop and pitcher. In 2009, he was drafted by the Florida Marlins. Currently, he is enjoying life in California with his wife and two daughters. (Courtesy of Jessica Carrillo.)

Albert A. Suchil is seen here in his parents' backyard at 621 West L Street in Colton, California. His parents, Yrineo and Luz Suchil, came from Aguascalientes, México, in 1912 and settled in Colton. Albert was born in 1913 and was the fifth of fourteen children. He was an outstanding athlete at Colton High School, playing baseball, football, basketball, and track. After high school, he worked with the Civilian Conservation Corps during the Great Depression. He played on several Mexican American teams in the Inland Empire from the 1930s through the 1950s, including with the semi-professional Colton Mercurys. His father made homemade Mexican candy in the garage and sold it at the ballpark. Albert played ball in the military with a medics' team during World War II. He was known as "Dynamite" for his exceptional play on the diamond. (Courtesy of Dale Suchil.)

Albert A. Suchil (left) is seen here with Medic teammate Willie Kimoso holding the 1943 Southern California Army Air Forces championship trophy. Suchil served in the US Army Air Forces during World War II in the Pacific Theater as a sergeant medical technician. He received the American Campaign Medal, Asiatic Pacific Campaign Medal, Good Conduct Medal, and the World War II Víctory Medal. After his military service, Suchil returned to Colton, California, and in 1946, he married Esperanza (Hope) Delgadillo. They had four children, Van, Mark, Dale, and Jackie. He worked as a foreman in the blast unit at the Kaiser Steel plant in Fotana. He loved baseball and played with several local Mexican American teams. In 2016, the city of Colton honored him with both a military banner and induction into its Baseball Hall of Fame. (Courtesy of Dale Suchil.)

CERTIFICATE OF
ATHLETIC ACHIEVEMENT

Palm Springs High School

This is to Certify that

Victor Reyes

was given an award for achievement in

Baseball

for the season of 1954

COACH PRINCIPAL

Víctor Reyes was born in the Mexican American community in Palm Springs, California. He was a four-year varsity letterman in baseball at Palm Springs High School in the 1950s. He received the Alan Hall Award for Palm Springs High School athlete of the year in 1956 and won the 1958 batting title in the Springs Desert Softball League. (Courtesy of Víctor Reyes.)

Associated Students
California State Polytechnic College
KELLOGG-VOORHIS CAMPUS

Athletic Achievement Award

Estella Elias

is entitled to wear the Athletic Emblem of this College

Awarded for

Softball

For the Season of

1963 - 64

Chairman of Awards Board

Coach

Growing up in Pomona, California, during the 1950s, Estella Elías Acosta and her younger sister Lydia Elías Mulkey enjoyed playing ball. They played on an improvised field adjacent to the Elías home that their father, Pedro, kept up. Estella's mother, Virginia García Elías, played softball for the GAA at Valencia High School in Placentia. In 1963, Estella attended Cal Poly Pomona. She and her softball team members set the foundation for future women's sports at the university. (Courtesy of Estella Elías Acosta.)

Enrique "Kiki" Hernández was born in El Paso, Texas, in 1931. Father Amado Hernández served in the Pacific during World War II despite having eight children. He was a member of the ROTC at Belmont High School in Los Angeles and was drafted into the Army, finishing basic training at Fort Roberts, California. He was sent to Berlin during the height of the Cold War. Hernández played ball as a youth on a company softball team, and in the military. He and Connie reside in La Puente, California. He enjoys bowling every Wednesday. (Courtesy of Enrique "Kiki" Hernández.)

Henry "Hank" Ynostroza (second row, second from left) played Little League and Babe Ruth at Huntington Park High School, and semiprofessionally. In high school during the 1960s, he led the team in every major offensive category for three seasons and was given a tryout with the Dodgers. He played with Ann's Panthers at Ross Snyder Park in Los Angeles and for El Rey Chorizo in East Los Angeles. His father, Henry, loved to box and gained notoriety as one of the defendants in the infamous 1942 Sleepy Lagoon case. (Courtesy of Henry "Hank" Ynostroza.)

Fernie Vásquez (batting) was born in Upland, California, and was a hard-throwing, right-handed pitcher. He played shortstop and leadoff hitter. Fernie learned ball from his brothers Sonny and Agustin "Tin," who played semipro. He played Little League, Pony League, Colt League, in high school, and with the Cucamonga Mets and Upland Angels. He also played electric guitar for several bands in the Inland Empire. (Courtesy of Joe Romero.)

The San Gabriel Aztecas of the 1930s were a very powerful team. From left to right are (first row) Frank "Bear" Pérez, unidentified from Pasadena, Devorsio Acosta, unidentified from Pasadena, and Johnny Miller; (second row) Joe "Fish" Barreras, Frank Cabral, unidentified from Pasadena, T. Noriega, Juaquín Gradias, Dave Morales, and Danny Domínquez. The batboy is Johnny "Bear" Pérez. (Courtesy of the Barreras family.)

Carlos Salazar is greeted by teammates after hitting a three-run home run for the Pasadena Independent West Pasadena Little League in 1952. He hit the winning home run and was the winning pitcher in relief. His brother David played military ball in the Army in Sendai, Japan, when stationed there with the 225th Regiment, 40th Division. (Courtesy of Carlos Salazar.)

Johno Ramírez (second row, second from left) was 10 years old when this picture was taken in 1962. His father, Johnny Ramírez (third row, far right), was the coach of the Dodgers. They had just lost the Artesia Valley League minor-league division championship. Johnny was promoted to the major competition league, starting a string of winning seasons that included division championships, and became the first coach to win an All-Star game for the city of Artesia. (Courtesy of Eva Ramírez Santillán.)

This 1960s Knights of Columbus team on Catalina Island was outstanding. From left to right are (first row) Johnny Saldana, Chip Upton, Pat Hubbard, Neal Lyon, Pete Finney, Nano Romo, Gilbert Hernández, and Raúl Hernández; (second row) Richard Félix, Steve Burke, Rocky Stocksdale, John Deacon, Greg Harkness, Richard Mead, Bobby Johnson, and Joe "Lipe" Hernández (coach). Joe and Maria "Maul" Hernández have donated over 50 years sponsoring youth programs, and have nine children. (Courtesy of Marcelino Saucedo.)

There were several women's softball teams, especially during the winter months on Catalina Island. From left to right are (first row) Diane Leonardi, Maria "Maui" Hernández, Judy Jordan, Vergie Félix, Pat Hernández, and Janie Isanhut; (second row) Bunny Rinehart, Vickie Hernández, Trudy Saldana, Pam Gardner, Alice Hernández, Jackie McLeish, and Dean Phelps (coach). Mexican families settled on Catalina as far back as the 1890s. Since people of color weren't allowed to live in town, the Mexican people lived on the outskirts of Avalon. (Courtesy of Marcelino Saucedo.)

This 1930s–1940s Yakima team of Los Angeles included Gene Madrid Tautimes (first row, far left). Tautimes played baseball and softball throughout Los Angeles County, including with his compadre Trino Cervantes (not pictured), from Inglewood, on the Seals. The Seals played their home games at Wrigley Field in South Central Los Angeles. Tautimes lived with his wife, Isabel Tresierras Tautimes, and their children in the Burbank barrio. The 5 freeway and industrial buildings stand on the site of the old neighborhood. (Courtesy of Mary Jane Muro.)

Encarnación Arellano emigrated from Zacatecas, México, in the early 1950s, settling with his family in El Sereno on the Eastside of Los Angeles. He graduated from Woodrow Wilson High School, playing baseball and football. He enrolled at Los Angeles Technical Institute and worked at Cielito Lindo on Olvera Street and at the General Motors plant in Van Nuys. He organized Los Santos (the Saints), operating from 1964 through 1970. From 1970 to 2012, he umpired for Little League, high school, and adult baseball and softball leagues. He was a member of the CIF, American Softball Association, and the Los Angeles Municipal Sports and Recreation and Parks. Arellano assisted in training new umpires. (Courtesy of Liz González.)

Sergio Hernández (left) was born at St. Mary's Hospital in Boyle Heights, East Los Angeles, in 1948 and graduated from Huntington Park High School playing baseball. He played ball at East Los Angeles Junior College and was on the magazine staff of *Con Sofos*, creating the cartoon strip *Arnie & Porfi*. He met his wife, Diane Velarde, on the CSUN campus. In 1970, Hernández and three other artists painted the first Chicano-themed mural at UCLA. He graduated in 1976, receiving a degree in Chicano studies and art. He joined the Los Angeles County Probation Department and retired as an investigator with the public defender's office. His father, Emidio, and his two brothers Sergio and Manuel (right) were outstanding ballplayers at Jefferson High and all played minor-league ball in the 1940s. (Courtesy of Sergio Hernández.)

Jenny Velarde Camacho (second row, right) was born in 1931 in Santa Fe, New México. Her family settled in Van Nuys, where she graduated from San Fernando High. She had three children, Diane, Michael, and Jimmy. Chris Díaz Puga (first row, far left) played on this 1940s team sponsored by the Los Angeles County Probation Department. Diane attended Guardian Ángel Church in Pacoima and graduated from San Fernando High and CSUN. She taught at San Fernando High for 33 years and was active with the East Los Angeles Walk-Outs, the farmworkers boycott, and La Raza Unida Party in Crystal City, Texas. (Courtesy of Diane Hernández.)

Eric Chavarria was born in Redlands, California. He played in Little League, Pony League, and Colt League. He played several positions, and his fastball was timed at 70 miles per hour in Colt League. Chavarria was a member of All-Star teams and played freshman ball at Redlands High School. He was a very good hitter. He moved to Las Vegas, Nevada, and is the nephew of Joe Romero, a legendary player from the Pomona Valley. (Courtesy of Joe Romero.)

Eddie Martínez played for the Claremont, California, Barons and the Upland Angels. He played shortstop and catcher for the Angels until he retired in 1964. The Angels traveled twice to Tijuana, México, for games. He and Joe Romero played together on the Barons and Mets. Martínez played third base with the Mets, including a game against the Upland American Legion. In that game, Sonny Vásquez move from third base to the mound, and Martínez played third base. It was a hard-fought game, and ultimately the Mets beat Upland by the score of 3-2. (Courtesy of Joe Romero.)

John "Choppers" Lemos was born in 1993, the youngest son of John Lemos. The younger John played with the Chino Little League and travel ball with the Chino Titans, coached by his father and Joe Keller. The Titans played the Hall of Fame Cooperstown Tournament in New York and two Triple Crown World Tournaments in Colorado, and they were four-time champions at the Spring National Tournaments in Tucson, Arizona. He played ball at John Glenn High School in Norwalk, California, and eventually played at Orange Coast College and Citrus Community College. He now plays recreational ball with his old high school and college teammates. (Courtesy of John Lemos.)

James A. Escoto was born in Montclair, California, and played ball throughout his youth, including T-ball, minors, majors, and All-Star teams. In a District 23 championship game, he hit three home runs. He played on the Chino High School freshman, junior varsity, and varsity baseball teams. (Courtesy of Joe Romero.)

Christina Castro started playing sports when she was four, including soccer, softball, volleyball, basketball, and tae kwon do. She played volleyball and softball at Mater Dei High School in Santa Ana, California. She was a member of the choir, performing in Florida, Germany, Austria, and Italy. She attended St. Joseph School in Placentia, serving on the student council. In 2019, Castro attends California State University at Fullerton, where she is a member of Sigma Kappa sorority and participates on her sorority's sports teams. Her grandfather Charles Santillán served with the US Army in Germany in the 1960s, while her great-grandfather Carlos Santillán served in World War II. (Courtesy of Stephanie Santillán Ramírez.)

Gabriela Ramírez, the younger sister of Christina Castro, also played a variety of sports. She currently plays soccer and softball year-round. She is active in student government at St. Joseph School and recently earned her Bronze Award with the Girl Scouts. Her mother, Stephanie Ramírez, played sports at St. Boniface School and Connelly High School in Anaheim, where she played volleyball, basketball, and softball. She enjoys watching and coaching her three daughters. Stephanie coached an undefeated volleyball team in 2018 at St. Joseph. (Courtesy of Stephanie Santillán Ramírez.)

The San Diego Hernández brothers, from left to right, are Larry, Manuel, Chapo, and Goyo. It was difficult to find ballplayers during World War II. Because of a heart murmur, Manuel was classified as 4F. The former San Diego High School prep star became the Padres' starting left fielder on Opening Day 1944. When the local Selective Service office learned this, he was drafted into the Army. Hernández fought in the Battle of the Bulge and was killed by enemy fire while crossing the Rhine in March 1945. He remains the only Padre to have made the ultimate sacrifice for his country. (Courtesy of Tina Hernández.)

The Vásquez brothers (from left to right) Sonny, Fernie, and Tin, played in Ontario, California. Sonny pitched and played the infield on one team, while Fernie and Tin played on another Ontario team. All three played Little League, senior league, pony and colt leagues, and high school. After high school, they played for the Cucamonga Mets, with Sonny pitching and playing third base, Fernie playing shortstop, and Tin playing third base and the outfield. In 1964, Joe Romero organized a team to play against the Upland American Legion team, winners of the American Legion World Series tournament in Little Rock, Arkansas. Romero's team won 3-2. (Courtesy of Joe Romero.)

1 2 3 4 5 6 7 8 9 10 11 12 13 14 15 16 17 18

NOTE: This ticket will be forfeited and player barred from the tournament if used by any party other than the one whose name appears on the first line.

California State Baseball Tournament

1939 TORRANCE CITY PARK DIAMOND JULY 8 - 30 **1939**

PLAYER'S PASS 165

ISSUED TO Alfonso O'Rozco

TEAM Carpenters Union #25

SIGNATURE Dale V. Riley

ISSUED BY Torrance Chamber of Commerce Tournament Committee

SANCTIONED BY NATIONAL SEMI-PRO BASEBALL CONGRESS

Alonzo Orozco was born in 1908 in Tucson, Arizona Territory, the ninth of 13 children to Rafael Orozco and Manuela Macías. During the Depression, Alonzo worked in the Civilian Conservation Corps in California. He enlisted in the US Merchant Marines during World War II and was assigned to the USS *Wisconsin* as a gunner. Alonzo and his wife, Rosemarie Salazar, started a family with two sons, Alonzo Jr. and Joseph, and a daughter, Elisa. This card was issued to Alfonso O'Rozco from the Carpenters Union 25 team. His name is spelled incorrectly. (Courtesy of the Orozco family.)

Alfonso Olmos

as been presented this certificate for outstanding athletic achievement
nd successfully meeting the requirements in citizenship and scholarship.

Coach

Commissioner of Athletics

Alfonso Olmos (first row, far left) was drafted by the San Francisco Giants and the Army in 1968, completing his training at Fort Ord, California, where he played ball before being shipped to Vietnam with the 506th Regiment, 101st Airborne Division. Alfonso kept his Giants contract inside his helmet. He was killed on July 19, 1969. The movie *Hamburger Hill* depicts the battle in which he lost his life. (Courtesy of David Olmos.)

Ray Armenta (second row, second from right) played at McKinley Junior High School in 1926. Ray and his three brothers, Tony, Paul, and Óscar, were outstanding players. In 1932, the four brothers played for La Alianza Mexicana, a semiprofessional team in Los Angeles. This was the only time they all played on the same team. The family fled the Mexican Revolution and eventually settled in Los Angeles in 1922. (Courtesy of Bea Armenta Dever.)

Isabella Ramírez started playing sports at the age of five including softball and soccer. She enjoyed taking ballet lessons. Like her sister, Gabriela, she plays soccer and softball year-round, plays the piano, and is a member of the Girl Scouts. She enjoys being in school plays and writes stories. She has two sisters, Christina and Gabriela. Her uncle, Steven Santillán, was born in 1974 and graduated from Servite High School and the University of Southern California. He played youth baseball, basketball, and flag football and was the captain of the swim team in high school. (Courtesy of Stephanie Santillán Ramírez.)

6

Coast to Coast

Since the 1970s, Mexican migration has received a tremendous amount of attention, especially in the Deep South and Midwest. Countless news stories and scholarly research have attempted to explain why Mexicans have continued settling in parts of Louisiana, Georgia, Alabama, Mississippi, Tennessee, Virginia, Kansas, Nebraska, and Iowa. This Spanish-speaking exodus is deeply rooted, dating back almost 170 years. In the late 1800s, a few Mexicans moved into the Deep South states, picking cotton. Since Texas shares a border with Louisiana, it became a gateway into other Southern states.

The Midwest witnessed a significant flow of Mexicans seeking employment and refuge from political violence decades ago. In 1850, Wisconsin counted nine Mexicans and Illinois 50, while the first Mexicans settled in Minnesota in 1886. In 1900, there were 56 Mexicans in Michigan and 1,000 in Chicago. One major explanation is geography, since Texas is closer to these Midwest and Southern states than to California. San Antonio, Texas, is closer to Kansas City and Chicago than to Los Angeles, and Lubbock, Texas, is only 180 miles from Garden City, Kansas. El Paso, Texas, has been historically the immigration doorway into Oklahoma and Kansas and points further north.

In many ways, Mexicans entering the United States—whether in 1850, 1950, or 2019—have shared similar experiences, with both the welcome mat and outright hostility. Regardless of when they arrived, religion has been the key to their survival. When Mexicans first arrived in towns, they built a church, typically named after Our Lady of Guadalupe. Today, many Catholic churches and other religious faiths have Spanish-language services for new immigrants. The second action that Mexican newcomers undertook was constructing baseball diamonds. Baseball was very popular in México (and still is) and therefore was not foreign to the newcomers. The Catholic Church generally sponsored baseball teams, fittingly named Guadalupanas.

Mexicans play *futbol* (soccer) basketball, and North American football, but baseball and softball are still the most popular. From coast to coast, there are teams, leagues, and tournaments dominated by recently arrived immigrants. And like the generations of early Mexican baseball and softball teams since the 1870s, Spanish is still the preferred language at games, Mexican music is still heard in the bleachers, Mexican food and drink are still sold, and most importantly, most fans still attend church services before the game.

Ray Aguilar Chevron sponsored the 1971 Creighton Baseball League youth team in Phoenix, Arizona. Aguilar was a close friend to the team's coach, Tommy Nuñez Sr. From left to right are (first row) Johnny "Chaco" Martínez, Ernie Domínguez, Ángel Domínguez, "Doo-Doo" Facio, Danny Broderick, Tommy Martínez, and Sal Paletta; (second row) Henry Facio, unidentified, Jim Skelly, Tommy Nuñez Jr., Mike Anderson, Tony Chiarello, and Johnny Rodríguez; (third row) Tommy Nuñez Sr. (Courtesy of the Nuñez family.)

Tommy Nuñez Jr. progressed through neighborhood baseball leagues, establishing himself as a homegrown talent as he reached college. After playing baseball and graduating from St. Mary's High School, He played two seasons at Phoenix College, the local junior college, from 1978 to 1980. He then played for Grand Canyon College (now Grand Canyon University) in Phoenix from 1980 to 1982. Nuñez played shortstop and helped the Antelopes win back-to-back National Association of Intercollegiate Athletics (NAIA) titles. He broke the NAIA World Series stolen base record in 1981 with seven and received the NAIA World Series Golden Glove Award in 1982. (Courtesy of the Nuñez family.)

Tommy Nuñez Jr. and his wife, Joanie, had four children, each of whom grew up playing baseball or softball. Tommy is seen here in 1996 coaching three of his kids (from left to right), Alex (five), Kaitlyn (three), and Michael (five). His children, like many of their friends and neighbors, were raised playing sports in local recreation leagues, including the Tempe YMCA. Coaches and other volunteers were often parents or other family members. Recreation leagues provided a cost-friendly, communal way to get kids involved from an early age and helped them develop their skills by fostering competitiveness, teamwork, and healthy behavior. (Courtesy of the Nuñez family.)

Alex (left) and Michael Nuñez became fans of the Arizona Diamondbacks during the team's inaugural season in 1998. Before the Diamondbacks, many Arizonans had allegiance to other teams, but the birth of a new local team forced baseball fans to realign their rooting interests. The Diamondbacks played games at Bank One Ballpark (now Chase Field) in Phoenix. They became the youngest franchise to win the World Series in 2001, defeating the New York Yankees in seven games. (Courtesy of the Nuñez family.)

Coaching careers often begin when playing careers end. Kaitlyn Nuñez played varsity softball at Corona del Sol High School in Tempe. Upon graduating from high school, she ended her playing career and took time to tutor her younger sister Analiese in the fundamentals of the game. Kaitlyn had been coached by her father, Tommy Nuñez Jr., throughout youth softball and assisted him in coaching her younger sister in 2011. Analiese joined a division of JetHawks T-Ball based out of Kiwanis Park in Tempe, playing with many friends from school and other local community members. (Courtesy of the Nuñez family.)

DANCE

Given by

Silvis Aztecs Baseball Club

EAGLES HALL, EAST MOLINE

MUSIC BY PAULLGAMINO & HIS ORCHESTRA

Saturday Sept, 5th

DANCING 9:00 to 1:00

Don't Miss the Double Header Sunday, Sept. 6
at John Deere Diamond, East Moline

1st Game 12:30 .... Aztecs vs. Chicago All-Stars
2nd Game .... Aztecs vs. Blue Island Latinos

Everybody Invited — Dance Admission $1.50

Refreshments

Circulars Donated by RAY COMPOS, MOLINE

Mexican national holidays (*Las Fiestas Patrias*) often included ball games as part of the festivities. Silvis, Illinois, is part of the Quad-Cities region along with Moline, Illinois, and Davenport and Bettendorf, Iowa. Mexicans came to this area working mainly on the railroads. The most celebrated memorial of Mexican American patriotism is in Silvis; nearly 130 of its young men fought in World War II, Korea, and Vietnam. In memory of all these veterans, including eight killed in action, Hero Street was dedicated on October 31, 1971, after a long struggle to recognize the military contributions of Mexican Americans. This poster is from the early 1950s. (Courtesy of Joe Terronez.)

Isabel Ramírez was born in Hartland, Kansas, in 1934. His parents, José and Maria, settled in Albuquerque, New México, in 1910. His father worked for the Burlington Northern, Union Pacific, and Santa Fe Railroads as a track laborer. His mother raised 10 children. The family eventually settled in Scottsbluff, Nebraska, where his mom's parents worked in the sugar beet fields. Isabel played centerfield throughout his career, including with the American Legion, Southeast Recreation Center, Mission League, Mitchell Eagles, and various softball teams and leagues. He played ball until 1970. (Courtesy of Isabel Ramírez.)

In the early 20th century, Mexicans in South Chicago rallied around organizations that helped open recreational spaces and opportunities despite ethnic prejudice, gender inequalities, and lack of resources that created physical, economic, and psychological boundaries. Leaders emerged and used their sports teams and organizations as vehicles to push beyond their externally imposed boundaries and claim their rights as residents of this country. Mexicans were not able to use Bessemer Park until the late 1920s. (Courtesy of Michael Innis-Jiménez and the Southeast Chicago Historical Society.)

The men and women and boys and girls who played or organized sports teams were important actors in shaping Mexican South Chicago's physical environment and in improving individual and community welfare during the Great Depression. Players may have been struggling to survive, but when they put on uniforms and competed against teams from outside of South Chicago, they represented their community. (Courtesy of Michael Innis-Jiménez and the Southeast Chicago Historical Society.)

Infielder Leopoldo Martínez (first row, far left) was born in Chihuahua, México, in 1920, and played for teams in Texas, México, and California from the 1930s through the 1960s. He immigrated to the United States and eventually settled in La Puente, California. He even competed in Nicaragua, where he played in the 1948 Amateur Baseball World Series (also known as the Baseball World Cup) as a member of the Mexican national team. (Courtesy of the Leopoldo Martínez family.)

Dave Salazar (second from right) played for the Mesa Miners in the Arizona League in the 1920s against teams from Globe, Bisbee, Glendale, Tucson, and Phoenix. He also pitched in the Texas-Arizona League with El Paso and later in 1924 in the Pacific Coast League with the San Francisco Seals. His children, grandchildren, and great-grandchildren have made a name for themselves playing ball throughout California and overseas. (Courtesy of Carlos Salazar.)

Albert Valtierra stands by a car at N.R. Crozier Technical High School in Dallas, Texas, where he graduated in 1966. He was born in Somerset, Texas, in 1947 to Francisco and Serapia Valtierra. His three siblings are Frank, Alice, and Rosemary. The family moved to Dallas in 1956. Albert retired from Southwestern Bell in 1999 and has been a community activist for over 40 years. He has been involved with several nonprofit organizations, serving in leadership roles with these groups. He played Little League baseball, where he attempted to be a left-handed pitcher. (Courtesy of Albert Valtierra.)

Albert Valtierra took high school classes in photography. He served in the US Air Force from 1967 to 1971, assigned to the 45th Reconnaissance Squadron, 460th Tactical Reconnaissance Wing, headquartered at Tan Son Nhut Air Base in Saigon from 1969 to 1970. Valtierra processed photographs taken by pilots flying over enemy territory to determine the precise location of troops for the next round of strategic bombing. The training camera he is holding is the same type he used in class to take a photograph of John F. and Jackie Kennedy only minutes before the president was assassinated on November 22, 1963. (Courtesy of Albert Valtierra.)

John Fraire is seen here in 1964 in his Gary, Indiana, uniform. Fraire takes pride that at the age of six, he played real baseball, not T-ball. He played in the farm league on Saturdays. His father coached him and his four brothers. Baseball was an integral part of his life and identity. John's mother, Gloria, was one of the first Mexican women in Indiana Harbor to play varsity sports at East Chicago Washington High School. (Courtesy of John Fraire.)

Baseball in Indiana Harbor in East Chicago, Indiana, flourished from the 1920s through the 1940s. Local baseball teams played key roles helping the community develop both its *Mexicanidad* (Mexican identity) and American identity. Rather than facing the choice of becoming either more Mexican or American, members of the community could and did develop both identities. Seen here is the Los Gallos (the Roosters) team around 1938. (Courtesy of John Fraire.)

Marge Villa Cryan is seen here catching in Havana, Cuba, during the 1940s. She was born in 1925 in Montebello, California, on her father, Jay's, 20-acre farm. Her siblings were Eleanor, Ernie, and Tony. Her playground was the clay pit of the Simon Brickyard. She was a self-proclaimed tomboy and loved playing ball with her brothers. She later played for the Forum Club of East Los Angeles, Greenfield Service, Garvey Stars, and Crew Oldsmobile in Fullerton. (Courtesy of Jonathan C. Reed.)

Marge Villa Cryan (11th from left) played ball in Managua, Nicaragua, during the 1940s. In 1943, during World War II, she wanted to join the Women Air Force Service Pilots, but her parents would not allow it. Instead, she worked at the US Rubber plant (now the Citadel) as a "Rosita the Riveter." In 1946, she was invited to join the All-American Girls Professional Baseball League (made famous in the 1992 film *A League of Their Own*), playing for the Kenosha, Wisconsin, Comets through 1954. (Courtesy of Jonathan C. Reed.)

Marge Villa Cryan (first row, fourth from right) played in Caracas, Venezuela. She was an outstanding catcher for the All-American Girls Professional Baseball League, making several All-Star teams. These teams traveled throughout Central and South America, Cuba, and México. In her rookie year with Kenosha in 1946, Cryan made history when she drove in nine runs and collected 11 total bases, setting two single-game league records that would never be surpassed. At the age of 94, she still participates in baseball events highlighting Mexican American women trailblazers on the diamond. (Courtesy of Jonathan C. Reed.)

Field of Dreams

This is the 16th book in the Arcadia Publishing series on the far-reaching history of Mexican American baseball and softball in the United States and beyond. The last chapter of each book is entitled Field of Dreams. The initial idea for this chapter was to show former players in the ninth inning of their lives as a means of honoring them. Eventually, other related subjects including ballfields named after players and coaches, photographs of multi-generational family members, and pictures of old gloves, bats, uniforms, trophies, and other memorabilia were added.

The very first Field of Dreams photograph in 2011 showed Saul Toledo holding a bat and wearing his Carmelita Chorizeros baseball cap at a local park near his home. Toledo was known as "Mr. Baseball of East Los Angeles," probably doing more than anyone to promote community baseball. Sadly, less than a month after the picture was taken, he passed away at the age of 90 in September 2010. More than 200 photographs have been highlighted in the Field of Dreams chapters.

Another essential part of the Field of Dreams chapter is to document the many public and community events paying homage to these remarkable players, coaches, umpires, and others who have brought immense honor and boundless pride and joy to their fans, families, friends, and neighborhoods. These tributes are taking place nationwide and much more frequently. In 2018, old-time ballplayers were honored in Greeley, Colorado; Newton, Kansas; East Los Angeles, California; and Kansas City, Kansas, and Missouri. It is important to record these events for future generations.

Sadly, many Mexican Americans related to the game have gone on to the big diamond in the sky. In the 1951 film *Angels in the Outfield*, the voice from heaven refers to its team as the "heavenly nine." In a previous Field of Dreams chapter, a reference was made to the film *Field of Dreams*. It is the *esperanza* (hope) of the Latino Baseball History Project that these "angels" in the spiritual outfield are once again playing the game that they loved so much and that each of them is a guardian angel to the countless youth still playing on the diamonds where their ancestors once roamed.

In November 2016, family members, friends, and community residents came by St. Anne's Catholic Church in Santa Monica to enthusiastically support siblings Alicia Serra Stevens and Ray Serra Jr., coauthors of a chapter on Santa Monica baseball and softball in *Mexican American Baseball in Ventura County*. From left to right are (first row) Gloria Serra Willis, Alicia Serra Stevens, Ray Serra Jr., and Armida Barron Murray; (second row) Manuel Serra, Frances Galván, Manuel López, and Elizabeth López; (third row) Michael Serra and Rubén Casillas. (Courtesy of the Serra family.)

At a second Santa Monica book signing in November 2016, several former players were present at the Moose lodge celebrating the chapter written by Alicia Serra Stevens and Ray Serra Jr. From left to right are (first row) Ray Serra Jr., Tommy Gómez, David Martínez, Sal Hernández, José Verduzco, and Manuel Serra; (second row) Rick Redondo, Paul Gómez, Anthony Romero, Rubén Casillas, and Larry Arreola. (Courtesy of the Serra family.)

The Serra children, proud of their father's achievements, created posters documenting Mexican American baseball images from Santa Monica teams, coaches, and players. They are seen at a book-signing event at St. Anne's Catholic Church in November 2016 beside the posters they created. From left to right are Ray Serra Jr., Alicia Serra Stevens, and Manuel Serra, the children of Ray Serra. (Courtesy of the Serra family.)

From left to right are Rebecca García Prieto, Rick Prieto, and Sandra Prieto. The family refer to themselves as "the home team," supporting each other through life's joys, sacrifices, and adversities. Rick earned his bachelor of arts in history from Loyola Marymount University (LMU) and master of arts in physical education and coaching from Azusa Pacific University. Rebecca's employment history includes assistant bursar at LMU, Rotary District 5280 administrator, and positions with the Culver City Unified School District. Sandra is wearing her CCHS volleyball jersey; she served as team captain and was a scholar-athlete. She proudly followed in her father's footsteps by earning her bachelor of arts in history and secondary education from LMU. She is currently teaching history and coaching volleyball. In 2014, she was named Wish Charter Middle School's Teacher of the Year. (Courtesy of Fred Altieri.)

Former CCHS Centaurs reunite at their beloved field. These Mexican Americans contribute their precious time, baseball knowledge, and love of the game to coach future players. From left to right are Jesse Plasencia (class of 1978), Fr. Jacob (Botello) Levy (2000), Rick Prieto (1974), George Aceves Jr. (2012), Patrick Rincón (2009), Ryan Jiménez (2009), and Juan Cueva (1989). Jacob, Ryan, Patrick, and George all played for Rick and later returned to coach with him. (Courtesy of Fred Altieri.)

In May 2017, members of historic San Fernando Valley families met for lunch. They included former players Pete Prieto (third from left) and Joe Escalante (fifth from left). Pete and brother Eddie Prieto played on the Pacoima Athletic Club and Athletics during the 1940s. Joe Escalante and brother Albert played on 1930s Pacoima teams. Also present were Irene Vaiz (third from right) and Alice Almeida (second from right). Irene Vaiz's husband, Manuel, played in San Fernando for decades, including for Van Nuys General Motors UAW teams. (Courtesy of Christopher Docter.)

These scenes at Culver City high school include, clockwise from top left, the nostalgic wooden scoreboard, replaced by a state of the art scoreboard from the generous donation of Thomas and Leah Schiffer, owners of Grey Block Pizza; the backstop of the new softball complex, erected in 2015 as a permanent home for Centaur softball players and the enjoyment of their fans; coach Rick Prieto dragging the infield on his cart to ensure the safety of the players and beauty of the field; and a mobile classroom, named the "Clubhouse" brought in to replace the "Hut" as the locker room for the baseball program. The baseball and softball programs truly have fields of dreams now. (Courtesy of Rebecca García-Prieto.)

Virginia Ruiz Durazo (left) and Lillian Ruiz Baeza visit in 2017. Along with their sisters Beatrice and Alice, they formed the cornerstone of the 1930s and 1940s Van Nuys women's softball teams. Multiple teams played on a vacant lot at the corner of Delano Street and Cedros Avenue every weekend. The family lived in the Simons Brickyard community in present-day Montebello before moving to Van Nuys in the San Fernando Valley. (Courtesy of Christopher Docter.)

In the foreground, from left to right, Alicia Serra Stevens, Raymond "Ray" Serra Jr., and Pinney García Jr. chat at the Mexican American Baseball program at the Museum of the San Fernando Valley in February 2017. Their fathers, Raymond Serra Sr. and Pinney García Sr., were teammates on the San Fernando Missions throughout the 1940s. The younger Pinney continued the family athletic tradition, playing with San Fernando Little League and baseball and football at San Fernando High School. He later competed on the UAW softball team at the Van Nuys General Motors plant. In the background stand his cousins Beverly García Manasse and Jim García. Their father, James "Jimmy" García, played baseball for the Pacoima Athletic Club in the late 1940s. (Courtesy of the Museum of the San Fernando Valley.)

Toñita's Restaurant deserves a special place in the history of Los Angeles restaurants and baseball. From 1961 until 1986, the Westlake district establishment hosted a who's who of Latino major-league players, musicians, and actors. The restaurant was founded by Antonia Fernández, whose family had moved from Puerto Rico to New York to Los Angeles, and specialized in Puerto Rican and Cuban cuisine. Seen here in January 2018 are Antonia's daughter and grandson Hilda Fried and Héctor Meneses with photographs and other memorabilia from Toñita's. (Courtesy of Héctor Meneses.)

On January 27, 2018, a book signing and photograph collection event took place at the Santa Maria, California, library. The picture gathering was for an upcoming book on Mexican American baseball and softball in the Santa Maria Valley. Seen here from left to right are Eddie Navarro, Richard A. Santillán, Al Ramos, and Ernie Corral. Both Navarro and Ramos have contributed previous chapters to this series on the history of baseball and softball in Santa Maria, Guadalupe, Lompoc, Los Alamos, Santa Barbara, Carpentaria, Goleta, Sisquoc, and other local communities. All four are coauthors for the upcoming book. (Courtesy of Richard A. Santillán.)

In July 2018, Newton, Kansas, hosted its 70th annual softball tournament, drawing teams from surrounding states to one of the oldest softball tournaments in the country and the highly anticipated traditional old-timers game. In no particular order are Manuel Jaso, Ralph Palacio, Fortunato Bonilla, Tony Jaso, Harvey Del Castillo, Donald Díaz, Joe Waco, Brian Padilla, Paul Hernández, Ralph Pacheco, Anthony Vieyra, Luis López, Stan Ramos, Paul Vega, Chris Rodríguez, Tony De La Torre, John Torrez, Greg Escobar, Mario Escobar, Scotty Gómez, Ron Escobar, Tony Agusto, ? Salas Sr., and Chris González. (Courtesy of Richard A. Santillán and Gene T. Chávez.)

In 2018, an event was held in Greeley, Colorado, saluting former and current players. From left to right are (first row) Kelvin McMillian (coach), John Barns, Char Rucobo, Dwight Steele, Abe García, Sam López, Jacoby Barnhill, Nudy López, Bud Anderson, Robert Ferguson, Don Stumf, Verl Timm, Arnoldo Maltos-García, Don Rolf, and Louis Zuñiga; (second row) Chris Mohr, Josh Archer, Issac Bracken, Braydon Peif, Nic Laporta, Travis Lechman, Rafael Villela, Ty Montgomery, Cody Beck, Sean Kelson, Luke Vargas, Daniel Moore, Chris DeSousa, John Magruder, and Cody Lawson. (Courtesy of Gabriel and Jody López.)

Rod Martínez is seen with sister Christina "Tina" Martínez Trujillo at the 70th annual Newton, Kansas, softball tournament in early July 2018. Tina and her husband, David, hosted Rod and Richard Santillán. Tina graduated from Newton High School and worked as a beautician. She is very active in community affairs and the local Catholic church. Their father, Ray, and uncle Jay Martínez were outstanding players throughout the Midwest. (Courtesy of Richard A. Santillán.)

Jessica Carrillo was born in San Bernardino, California. Her family moved to Bloomington in 1993. Even though she played Little League for only one year, baseball has played a major part in her life for over 20 years thanks to her father and brother, who love the sport. She received her associate of arts in early childhood education from Riverside Community College and her bachelor's degree in liberal studies from California State University at San Bernardino. She will obtain her master's degree in 2019 from the University of Redlands. She is pictured in 2018 in front of the old scoreboard where she played Little League. (Courtesy of Jessica Carrillo.)

Anthony González served as the El Pueblo director of Olvera Street. He currently serves as president of the Route 66 Inland Empire California group restoring the Cucamonga Service Station with the goal of converting the site into a museum. The organization sponsors monthly events highlighting the valuable contributions of Mexican Americans to American society, as seen here in January 2018. From left to right are (first row) unidentified, Richard Vásquez, and Al Vásquez; (second row) Irene C. González, Christina González Magoni, Mike and Patti García, Anthony González, Mary Rivera González, and Al Ledesma. Mary is the mother of Anthony and Christina. (Courtesy of Richard A. Santillán.)

BIBLIOGRAPHY

Arbena, Joseph L. "Sport, Development, and Mexican Nationalism, 1920–1970." *Journal of Sport History* 18, no. 3 (Winter 1991).

"Aztecs Name Sam Peraza Baseball Coach." San Diego State University Athletics. http://goaztecs.com/coaches.aspx?rc=4&path=baseball.

Bloom, John, and Michael Nevin Willard. *Sports Matters: Race, Recreation, and Culture*. New York, NY: New York University Press, 2002.

Cahn, Susan K. *Coming on Strong: Gender and Sexuality in Twentieth-Century Women's Sport*. Toronto, ON: Free Press, 1994.

Cerra, Julie Lugo. "Culver City Timeline: A Work in Progress." Culver City Historical Society. Last modified June 2014. www.culvercityhistoricalsociety.org/about/culver-city-timeline.

Chavez, Christina. *Five Generations of a Mexican American Family in Los Angeles: The Fuentes Story*. Lanham, MD: Rowman & Littlefield, 2007.

Galarza, Ernesto. *Spiders in the House & Workers in the Fields*. South Bend, IN: University of Notre Dame Press, 1970.

García, Juan R. *Mexicans in the Midwest: 1900–1932*. Tucson, AZ: University of Arizona Press, 1996.

Masters, Nathan. "When North Hollywood Was a Town Named Tuluca, or Lankershim." *Lost LA*. Los Angeles, CA: KCET, June 20, 2014.

Matthiessen, Peter. *Sal Si Puedes: Cesar Chavez and the New American Revolution*. New York, NY: Random House, 1969.

McCarthy, Dennis. "Dedicated Dads Build Their Own 'Field of Dreams.' " *Los Angeles Daily News*. September 11, 2014.

McWilliams, Carey. *Factories in the Fields*. Santa Barbara, CA: Peregrine Press, 1971.

Netzel, Chip. Culver City High School Centaurs Baseball Facebook page.

Ruebsamen, James, and Francis Palermo. *Sports Graphic*. Culver City High School, 1974.

Santillán, Richard. "Mexican Baseball Teams in the Midwest, 1916–1965: The Politics of Cultural Survival and Civil Rights." *Perspectives in Mexican American Studies*. Tucson, AZ: Mexican American Studies and Research Center at the University of Arizona, 2001.

Santillan, Richard A., et al. *Mexican American Baseball in Ventura County*. Charleston, SC: Arcadia Publishing, 2016.

Simon, Melissa. "From the Front Lines of the Pacific." *Simi Valley Acorn*, May 26, 2017.

"Yvonne Gutierrez Named to the UCLA Athletics Hall of Fame." May 29, 2013. http://uclabruins.com/sports/2013/5/29/208473256.aspx.

Latino Baseball History Project Advisory Board

www.ingramcontent.com/pod-product-compliance
Lightning Source LLC
LaVergne TN
LVHW081548100826
845153LV00004B/338

* 9 7 8 1 5 4 0 2 3 9 5 1 8 *